Thérèse, Faustina, and Bernadette

Three Saints

Who Challenged My Faith, Gave Me Hope, and Taught Me How to Love

Elizabeth Ficocelli

ave maria press AMP notre dame, indiana

The medal of St. Thérèse of Lisieux on the cover can be found at etsy.com/shop/MarysPrayers.

The medal of St. Faustina on the cover can be found at etsy.com/shop/Gwendysgems.

The medal of St. Bernadette on the cover can be found at www.etsy.com/shop/CalliopesWork.

© 2014 by Elizabeth Ficocelli

Founded in 1865, Ave Maria Press is a ministry of the United States Province of Holy Cross.

www.avemariapress.com

Paperback: ISBN-13 978-1-59471-374-3

E-book: ISBN-13 978-1-59471-375-0

Cover and text design by Katherine Robinson.

Printed and bound in the United States of America.

Library of Congress Cataloging-in-Publication Data
Ficocelli, Elizabeth.
Thérèse, Faustina, and Bernadette : three saints who challenged my faith, gave me hope, and taught me how to love / Elizabeth Ficocelli.
    pages cm
 ISBN-13: 978-1-59471-374-3 (pbk.)
 ISBN-10: 1-59471-374-X (pbk.)
 ISBN-13: 978-1-59471-375-0 (ebook)
 ISBN-10: 1-59471-375-8 (ebook)
 1. Spiritual life--Catholic Church. 2. Thérèse, de Lisieux, Saint, 1873-1897. 3. Faustina, Saint, 1905-1938 4. Bernadette, Saint, 1844-1879. 5. Ficocelli, Elizabeth. I. Title.
 BX2350.3.F533 2014
 282.092'52--dc23
                    2013038424

"With openness and candor, Elizabeth Ficocelli reveals her personal experiences of living the challenges of her Catholic faith. Her peace and joy come in meeting these challenges by embracing the cross though the grace of prayer and the sacraments, and by following the example of newfound friends—her favorite saints."

Mother Mary Assumpta Long
Prioress General
Dominican Sisters of Mary, Mother of the Eucharist

"Tender, honest, introspective, and deeply personal, this book provides beautiful witness to the loveliness and wonder of the feminine genius! Elizabeth Ficocelli, writing from the insightful perspective of a convert to Catholicism who seeks to understand and unpack the mysteries of her own spiritual journey, reminds us in this gem of a book that we should all seek to acquire friendship with the saints and grow in the theological virtues. I highly recommend this book!"

Rev. Donald Calloway, M.I.C.
Author of *Under the Mantle*

"*Thérèse, Faustina, and Bernadette* is more than a simple recounting of the lives of three spiritual giants. Noted author and speaker Elizabeth Ficocelli shares how the companionship of her 'journey partners' has profoundly influenced her. For those of us endeavoring along the path to heaven, Ficocelli unveils some of the major pieces we need to assemble our own spiritual puzzles. An enlightening read!"

Lisa M. Hendey
Author of *A Book of Saints for Catholic Moms*

"In *Thérèse, Faustina, and Bernadette*, Elizabeth Ficocelli openly shares the special companions she discovered along her own spiritual journey in the hope of aiding others."

Donna-Marie Cooper O'Boyle
Author of *Rooted in Love*

"Read it! Woman to woman, page to page, this book jumps out and brings holy saints to life as the personal, trustworthy friends they truly are—friends who show us the way they know well to the place we want to go—Heaven!"

Marlene Watkins
President and Founding Administrator
Our Lady of Lourdes Hospitality
North American Volunteers

"As a young girl, Elizabeth Ficocelli discovered a religious medal trampled in the dirt and tucked it away in her treasure box. Little did she know that medal would be the key to discovering her true feminine self. This is not just another saint book on virtue, my friends. Any woman who has ever struggled to find her place in the world will identify with Ficocelli's powerful story of faith, love, and hope as she invites us to encounter three spiritual 'big sisters' and come to know them as trusted friends."

Heidi Hess Saxton
Blogger at *A Rosary on My GPS*

"Prepare yourself. You're about to meet three women who are remarkable and accessible. Ficocelli bares her heart, shares her life, and weaves in three of the great women saints of the last one hundred years. You'll learn, you'll laugh, and you'll walk away changed—with three new friends."

Sarah Reinhard
Author of *A Catholic Mother's Companion to Pregnancy*

"Author Elizabeth Ficocelli's newest title is a beautiful, important, and timely reminder that we are all on journeys that begin here on earth and end when we take up residence in our heavenly home."

Cheryl Dickow
President of Bezalel Books

"Through this book, Ficocelli not only introduces us to three of her beloved girlfriends, she shares them with us in a beautifully personal way."

Patti Armstrong
Author of *Dear God, I Don't Get It*

"Elizabeth Ficocelli's books always engage the reader at once and throughout; this one is no exception. Here she relates her own coming-of-age story of adult conversion and the vital, active help she's received along the way from Thérèse, Faustina, and Bernadette. This is classic Ficocelli—clear, straightforward, and thought provoking."

Susan Heybour O'Keefe
Author of *What Does a Priest Do? What Does a Nun Do?*

To all the

women in my life

who walk this

spiritual journey

with me

CONTENTS

PREFACE

When I was eight years old, I heard the voice of God—at least that's how I can best describe it. I can remember distinctly the day it happened, what I was doing, and even where I was standing when I encountered that voice. It spoke a short but simple sentence into my heart—not my head or ears—through a pathway I had never known existed and with an authority that was unmistakable. The words were clear and to the point: "I have a special mission for you." Even as a little girl, I was not alarmed by the voice, though I had never experienced anything like it before. I was intrigued and sought to engage with it, to no avail. More than four decades later, I can still remember that voice as if it were yesterday. I can recall my feeling of awe and excitement and the sense of knowing that this was an important moment in my life.

This childhood incident would set me on a journey of discovery that continues to this day. Once I had learned that there was a mission out there for me, I was determined to find it. My journey would take me in surprising directions, including embracing a faith apart from my family upbringing. It would lead me from the big city to the suburbs, from a corner office to a minivan, and from private worship to publically proclaiming the faith. Along the way, I learned to be comfortable in my own skin as an authentic woman (once I found out what that was), despite that being an authentic woman goes against modern culture. I would also discover, amid the twists and turns, that I was accompanied on this journey. God had in store for me amazing heavenly helpmates who would be there to challenge my faith, give me hope, and teach me to love, which is ultimately what this book is all about.

The truth is that each of us is on a journey and each of us has mission. We have been sent on this journey by our God who knows us, loves us, and wants nothing more than to be intimately involved every step of the way. We may not know he's there or even want him there at times. Though we may be tempted to forget or forsake him, God—in his infinite love—will never abandon his children to walk this journey alone.

Our loving Father delights in all of his children, of course, but I'd like to believe that God delights in women in a special way. We are precious in his eyes, for as the Genesis story alludes, we are the crown of his creation. Did you ever wonder why God created Eve last? It was not because he forgot about her or because she wasn't special enough; it was because Eve was God's finishing touch on creation. God has created women with beautiful hearts, minds, souls—and yes, even bodies (though few of us are at ease with that concept). We are daughters of the king, and it is his great pleasure to whisper plans and promises into the hearts of his daughters—if our hearts are open to them. Daily he sprinkles our paths with clues and kisses of his undying love for us. His love gifts may be spectacular, such as an exploding sunset in the desert, or gentle and fleeting, such as the dance of a hummingbird. He prompts us through the challenges of life with fatherly compassion, with inspirations from scripture, in the testimonies of others also on the journey, in songs that lift our spirits or inspire a tear, and in the examples of spiritual heroes who have gone before us. In a real and poignant way, our Lord reveals his very being in the intimate encounter of his sacraments, particular the Eucharist, the heavenly food for our journey.

Because he designed us, God knows that women in particular are relational in being. We thrive on interacting with others. That's why he carefully selected the perfect journey partners—our friends, spouses, children, co-workers—to encourage us, teach us, and stretch us for the journey and our ultimate destination of heaven. These journey partners and the situations of our lives that weave us together serve a special purpose. They offer the opportunity for us to develop virtue—holy habits of thought and behavior that help us become more Christ-like to ourselves and others. Virtue makes us more loving, more lovable, and better able to carry out God's special plans and purposes (our mission) for each of our lives.

Our earthly companions, however, aren't the only helpers whom God offers us for our journeys. In a special way, he presents spiritual journey partners who are eager to share the walk with us. These saintly journey partners offer us heroic examples of virtuous living and personal intercession as we navigate our way through this often-messy adventure we call life. Just as we may seek the assistance of personal trainers for our bodies, mentors for our professional careers, and life coaches for times of transitions, spiritual journey partners are there to help us in our faith walk, sharing valuable lessons and insights along the way.

God has blessed my own walk of faith by introducing me to several companions for the journey, but three women saints have entered my life in powerful ways at important moments and have left indelible impressions on my soul. They are Thérèse of Lisieux (the Little Flower), Faustina of the Divine Mercy, and Bernadette of Lourdes. These devout women of faith overcame tremendous spiritual and sometimes physical hurdles to leave us with profound discernments about the life of faith. They are models of holy living who have challenged how I think, how I behave, and who I am. Most of all, they have helped me to develop into a more virtuous woman (though there is much work yet to be done in this area). Through their example, I am learning to use my God-given gifts and natural feminine qualities to have a more positive effect on those around me.

My three spiritual companions did not earn their designation as saints just because they saw visions or wrote literary masterpieces. They were singled out by the Church for their heroic virtue—their ability to hold fast to their faith, hope, and love through all kinds of tests and trials. They lived tragically short lives, and they lived one right after another. Bernadette (1844–1879) and Thérèse (1873–1897) lived in France while Faustina (1905–1938) lived in Poland, and their lives on earth were cut short by the same deadly disease: tuberculosis. At death, Bernadette was thirty-five, Thérèse was twenty-four, and Faustina was thirty-three.

Each of these saints lived during times of great strife and turbulence. The first two saw the effects of the French Revolution usurping the strong role of the Church in France, while Faustina witnessed secularism mature into godless socialism and the subsequent spread of communism and Nazism. Despite the tumult around them, these holy daughters remained steadfast in their faith, hope, and love, and now give us important encouragement as we contend with the escalating tensions of our own day.

Thérèse, Faustina, and Bernadette shared other qualities as well. Each had a passion for saving sinners and rescuing souls, a fear of losing God's friendship, a dedication to a Gospel-based path to holiness, and a total abandonment to the will of God. Internally they struggled—as we all do—with self-will and self-love. They suffered spiritual dark nights of the soul, in which God's consolations were removed for a time. Each went through a physical passion of sorts during a slow and agonizing death. Yet all three of these spiritual giants learned to offer their sufferings for the good of others, which strengthened their virtue and led them to experience authentic joy, deep peace, and the crowning of glory.

It occurred to me in recent years that while these three special saints embodied many virtues, each demonstrated one particular virtue that I believe truly defines her character. For Bernadette, this virtue is faith. She was grounded in faith from the beginning of her life despite illness and poverty. She maintained her faith in the face of persecution and ridicule when chosen by God to deliver heavenly messages of Our Lady to a world gone astray. Finally, She upheld it for the remainder of her life as she lived the messages of prayer, penance, and conversion as a powerful witness to the world.

Faustina is defined by hope. She courageously accepted the spiritual assignment from Jesus himself to be his "secretary of mercy" in the hope that his messages, which she had carefully recorded and conveyed, would reach the world and heal it. Regardless of the disbelief of many of her superiors concerning her heavenly mission, the growing despair throughout Europe as Hitler's troops were invading, and her prophetic awareness that the messages and devotion of Divine Mercy would initially be rejected, Faustina placed all her hope and trust in Jesus, confident that his mercy was the antidote to conquer the presence of evil.

For Thérèse, the virtue is love. She was nurtured in love from birth and was passionate in her love in return, whether it was for her family, for nature, or most especially for God. She learned to overcome her own self-love to love God in a new way—a little way—that became an accessible path for millions. At a time when many French Catholics ascribed to a misguided theology that emphasized sin and a final judgment from which few would escape, Thérèse discovered a good and loving God who yearned for the love of his children, not their fear. Thérèse's heroic love for God and her mission to help others love him as she did continues to have a major impact on people today.

Just as they were needed in the lifetimes of these brave and innovative saints, the virtues of faith, hope, and love are desperately needed in our world today. Consider for a moment where we would be without them. Without faith, people are left to turn inward on themselves where they ultimately find unhappiness and lack of fulfillment. Without hope, people eventually usher emptiness and despair into their lives. Without love, human hearts grow cold as mistrust, lack of empathy, and a general disconnect from others become the norm. What is the answer to this downward spiral? The solution lies within us. We are the ones who can bring healing to a hurting world by developing these powerful virtues within ourselves and watching their life-giving impact on the people and situations around us.

God knew I needed a lot of help to become more virtuous, so first he sent me Thérèse, who softened my heart and showed me how to love God and others better. Then he sent me Faustina, who showed me how to be a person of hope—despite life's many challenges, and to trust God in everything—above all in his mercy. Finally he sent me Bernadette, who helped me to put my hope into action with a bolstered faith to weather the storms of life and come through them a stronger person. I will be forever indebted to these spiritual companions for the ways they have shaped and guided me, and I am greatly comforted knowing that they will be there for me in times to come.

Because of this, when I was first approached about writing a book to introduce these three heroines of faith to an audience of women in order to inspire them in their own pursuit of virtue, I could think of nothing more appealing. However, when they asked me to make the book personal, I felt a bit apprehensive. How could my small and ordinary story as a struggling sinner and convert merit in any way to be told alongside of the accounts of these momentous saints? I trusted God had some sort of plan, but it definitely placed me outside of my comfort zone. Unlike other books I've written, this book began without a preconceived outline or blueprint. I had just a sense of knowing that if I could do it right, there was a story here worth telling.

Writing this book was, at times, like putting together a five hundred–piece jigsaw puzzle upside down, where I couldn't see the final picture. I was forced to go piece by piece, day by day, trying to discover what piece fit with what. As I reflect now on the image of an upside-down jigsaw puzzle, I notice that the image seems analogous to life itself, for only God sees the final picture of our journeys. Meanwhile, we need to content ourselves with working on our lives one piece at a time, living in the present moment, paying attention to subtle intricacies, and trusting that our labors will gain us the final vision God has marvelously designed for us.

Following the intuitions of my publisher, I have woven into the book parts of my own spiritual journey, which naturally is a process that continues to evolve. I hope that in sharing some of my brokenness, the ways God has softened and healed my hardened heart, and the insights and blessings he has imparted to me through my spiritual journey partners, you may find encouragement and support in your own spiritual journey. I pray that something in the following pages may help you discover and embrace who you are as an authentically feminine woman so that you, too, can bloom where you are planted, whether that be in a skyscraper in the city or in an SUV littered with French-fries and crayons. In the spirit of the New Evangelization to which our three most recent popes have called us, this book is an attempt to witness person-to-person the transformative effect God can have in our lives and the great freedom and happiness that comes with our "yes" to him, even when that "yes" is whispered in weakness. To be sure, this is not a yay-me book; it is a yay-God book, because in his great goodness, he has never given up on me, despite the many reasons I have given him to do so.

It is now my great joy in the following chapters to introduce you to my three spiritual companions, offering the story of the way they came into my life and the invaluable lessons they have taught me to grow spiritually and in virtue. Perhaps after reading this book, you may choose Thérèse, Faustina, and Bernadette as your spiritual journey partners, or perhaps they will point you to others from the vast treasury of saints the Church has to offer. Either way, I thank you for allowing their stories and mine to become a part of your spiritual adventure, until with God's grace we all meet face-to-face in our final destination of heaven.

November 1, 2012
The Solemnity of All Saints

Unsaintly Behavior

I emerged from Grand Central Terminal on a warm summer morning in 1982 like an ant scurrying out of a dark tunnel to the bright sunshine above. The familiar honks of taxicabs, shouts of construction workers, and the whine of a police siren welcomed me to the busy street. Freshly graduated from college, I was a proud resident of New York City, with the tiny room and absurd rent to prove it. More importantly, I was at last a full-time part of the city's bustling workforce. A throng of passing commuters on the sidewalk of 42nd Street swept me into its living river of humanity, and at once I was part of the moving mayhem. At the corner of the block, I turned north on Madison Avenue with my styrofoam cup of Zaro's coffee in one hand and my leather briefcase swinging confidently from the other.

The advertising agency that hired me was only a short walk from the terminal, and the Nike running shoes I wore with my pinstriped business suit carried me swiftly to my destination. With a feeling of liberation and empowerment, I pushed my way through the massive revolving glass doors at the entrance of my office building. I was a young business-woman on the way up the corporate ladder with a bright and bold future ahead of me. I had jockeyed myself into a good position at the start of my career by completing four work/study internships—all in Manhattan—by the time I graduated summa cum laude from the University of Bridgeport in Connecticut. This helped me bypass the expected secretarial route to attain the coveted role of assistant account executive at the young age of twenty-two.

My first full-time assignment in the Big Apple was working for an account group that handled liquor and cigarette clients. It wasn't the most creative work, but I was immensely grateful for the opportunity. Madison Avenue, in those days, was regarded as the Mecca of the advertising world, and I was delighted to be in the nucleus where great headlines happened. It didn't particularly bother me at the time to work on campaigns for alcohol and tobacco. I had nothing against a good drink once in a while, and I had smoked socially in college. My cigarette of choice as a co-ed was Virginia Slims, the brand that reminded me with each theatrical puff that I had come "a long way, baby."

A Man's World

The one thing I didn't consider when I signed on to work for liquor and cigarette accounts was that I would find myself working smack dab in the middle of a man's world. All three of the account executives I assisted were men, as were both the account manager and the group manager. As far as I can remember, most of the people above them were men, too, even though it was the age when women were supposedly beginning to shatter those glass ceilings.

Women were, in fact, getting new opportunities. However, to compete in the male-dominated business world in the early 1980s, a woman could easily find herself being forced to be "one of the guys." It was the cultural climate of the day to play down one's femininity at all costs. Consequently, my business suits were conservative in cut and in a bland array of subdued colors, much like the conservative sling-back pumps I would slip into once I reached my cubicle. You would never find me sporting ruffles, bows, or—heaven forbid—slit skirts or plunging necklines. I made painstaking efforts not to let being a woman among all those male colleagues get in the way of being a business professional. In my mind, other than a few body parts, I couldn't see anything my male colleagues had that I lacked. I had graduated college with honors, I had pre-graduation work experience, and I had the right New York City attitude—work hard to get ahead, because there were plenty of people eager to take my job.

Fear of being easily replaced was in fact a major motivator for men and women—but for a lot of women, it came at a cost. It made me (and I suspect many others) take things in stride that today make me cringe. The year 1982 was long before policies were put in place to protect people from harassment in the office, and the boys' club could sometimes get pretty ugly. There were times, for instance, when some of the men in my department made inappropriate jokes and remarks in my presence. It often seemed as though they were doing it to test me—to see if the new college kid was up to being "one of the boys." I decided to face the challenge and pretend not to notice, even chiming in at times with my own laughter. Magazines containing our current cigarette and liquor advertisements routinely came through the office mail, including copies of *Playboy* and *Penthouse*. It was not uncommon for young male account executives to be thumbing through these periodicals in the adjacent cubicles, their whistles and comments drifting over the thin fabric walls. When someone anonymously began pinning up the latest centerfolds on the walls of the conference room as "inspiration" for brainstorming sessions, I felt a line had been crossed. I didn't have enough courage then to lodge a formal complaint out of fear of losing my job, but my grumbling at the water cooler somehow got passed along the chain of command, and the pictures were taken down as mysteriously as they had gone up. It was a minor victory from my vantage point, but not one that earned me any great favor with the male bosses.

My interaction with our clients—again, mostly men—didn't help matters. While the account team was generally on better behavior during client visits, the clients didn't always reciprocate. Going out to business dinners after work often meant having to deal with tipsy men who wanted to kiss me goodbye instead of accepting my firm handshake. With each passing month, it was becoming painfully obvious that as much as I had come "a long way, baby," I had not exactly arrived, if arriving meant being respected for my talents. In my corner of the advertising world in the early 1980s, the good-old-boy network was in full swing, and I was not a part of it. I would never be a part of it, and before too long I began to wonder if I really wanted to be a part of it at all.

I conformed to the norms of the times in terms of attire, and I took my job performance seriously. I liked to work and did my job well. But interiorly, deep within the confines of my soul, a bitter discontentment was beginning to simmer. It would not go away, no matter how many accounts I helped win or advertising awards our team clinched. The long hours and heavy workload of my first full-time advertising job in Manhattan convinced me (within a relatively short time) that the entire big-city experience was not for me. I lost ten pounds that I couldn't afford to lose and was barely sleeping at night. There was nothing I dreaded more than the sound of the alarm clock on an early Monday morning to signal the start of a new workweek. The hectic city life seemed fitting for all the other women catching subways in their tweed suits and running shoes, but I began to yearn for a smaller work environment in the suburbs, where the workdays might be slower and shorter. Perhaps there, I thought, I would find contentment. So, for reasons of health and sanity, I packed my scant belongings and returned to Long Island, the place of my birth, to begin a new chapter in my career.

Inner Conflict

The decision to alter my career path did have some imme-diate benefits. For starters, the move from the city to the suburbs allowed me to make the transition from winning accounts to actually creating them. This would have been an impossible switch to make otherwise, at least within the same agency ("Once a 'suit' always a 'suit,'" the creatives would say about the account-management team.) I found the role of advertising copywriter to be better suited to my writing abilities than assistant account executive—a position in which I had spent most of my time drafting brand reports and marketing strategies. Copywriting was more fun and less demanding, and I was grateful for the change.

There still were some things about the work environ-ment that had not really changed all that much. Yes, there were significantly more women working in the various sub-urban agencies I would serve, but it seemed that the men still held the highest positions. The behavior in the office was tamer and more "politically correct," but every now and again there was a hint of the good-old-boy network. The norms for attire were a little more relaxed as well, but

I still couldn't help feeling that I was wearing a uniform of sorts, one more determined by my attitude and behavior than fashioned with the material covering my body. I found myself locked into a self-imposed prison of perpetually trying to be recognized as a person no different from my male counterparts and superiors. "Equality, equality, equality"—that had been a mantra drilled into my head since I was in high school. I was taught that women were equal to men, plain and simple. Why then, I puzzled, was I experiencing such a disconcerting sense of inequality?

Eventually it dawned on me that the discord I was feeling had less to do with the men in the office than it had to do with me. I'm not saying that inappropriate behavior should ever be tolerated in the office. It absolutely should not. But what I began to realize is that my greater conflict was an interior one, a battle between a false self I had created in order to succeed in the workplace and my true self. That true self was a woman, not a man. I had suppressed the woman within for so long that I had no idea how to find her or if I would even be able to recognize her once I did.

In Stark Contrast

Writing about the early years of my advertising career still causes me to feel a bit sweaty and nauseous. When I revisit the fear and anxiety I experienced in those days and my lack of joy and fulfillment in the role I played, I am tempted to wish those times had not happened. I think though, that in some way, it was a necessary experience that would allow me to appreciate more fully what God next wished to reveal to me on my journey.

Today, my work environment is vastly different from what it was in my early advertising days, and I can only shake my head when I think about it. I might as well have jumped into a spaceship and headed for a distant galaxy. For starters, I no longer battle commuter traffic via train, subway, or car. I simply pad across the carpet in our master bedroom to a turret-shaped projection overlooking our backyard, which has a small stream and just enough trees to make it feel like a forest. From this serene outpost with birdsong as a backdrop, I work. I no longer write catchy headlines and persuasive copy to sell gizmos and gadgets. I now craft books to evangelize Catholics of all ages; scripts for PowerPoint presentations that I give at Catholic conferences, parishes, and schools; and research questions for the priests, deacons, and religious sisters and brothers I interview for an Ohio-based Catholic radio program. In stark contrast to my former conference-room walls with the pinups, my office today is decorated with pictures of popes, statues of the Virgin Mary, and holy cards with relics from my favorite saints. Three in particular hold a place of honor—Thérèse of Lisieux, Faustina of the Divine Mercy, and Bernadette of Lourdes. Their portraits are taped to my computer, where they smile at me and offer me encouragement each time I sit down to do tackle the week's demands. This is my team now, my coworkers, and we all report to the same supervisor—our Heavenly Father—to produce works far more important than any I had ever done on Madison Avenue.

If you were to tell me back in those early years fresh out of college that I would one day come not only to embrace the Catholic faith, but be called upon to defend it and teach it to others through writing, speaking, and the broadcast media, I would have thought you were out of your mind. If you had told me that some of my greatest mentors would turn out to be three young women from a century ago who had never worked in an office, earned a paycheck, or won an award from their peers, I would have been convinced you were off your rocker. I guess that's just the kind of surprising way God can work in our lives once we begin to surrender our journey to him and chance to voyage into the deep.

In the following chapter, I'll pick up the story of my exodus from the big city and show you how God, through his holy book and his vicar of Christ, taught me something that I could never have learned from my business contemporaries or their slickest ad campaigns—what it means to be a truly authentic woman.

Authentic Femininity

Coinciding with my move from city to suburbs and my transition from the business side of advertising to the creative was another drastic change: my decision to abandon my nominal Protestantism and come into full communion with the Roman Catholic Church. As I will reveal in greater detail in chapter four, I think I was being primed in subtle ways from my childhood for this transition, but my prime impetus for actually making the change was my desire to marry my Catholic boyfriend whom I had met in college. Becoming Catholic turned my world upside down in ways I had not anticipated and forced me to reevaluate and reprioritize my life's direction. It is within this ancient faith—one that the modern world often labels as male dominated, archaic, and insensitive to the plight of women—that I encountered what I believe God had in mind when creating the female with her inherent dignity and her authentic femininity. Ultimately and quite ironically, it was the Church, not the tabloids, the talk shows, or the so-called sex-and-relationship experts that helped me resolve my inner conflict as a woman in a man's world.

Women of Scripture

Before my conversion, I had always been an avid reader, and that didn't change when I became Catholic. What changed was what I read. I traded paperback novels for papal encyclicals. I gave up bestsellers for books on the saints. I immersed myself in Catholic apologetics (the explanation and defense of the faith), supernatural phenomena, and devotions. Early on, I got the inspiration to read the Bible—the whole Bible, cover to cover. I wanted to experience God's book from beginning to end, to try to grasp the bigger picture of my new faith. A reader-friendly version of the scriptures called the *New Jerusalem Bible* had just been published, and I snatched up a copy. I kept it in a canvas bag and read it discreetly on my lunch hour, hoping no one at the office would notice, lest I be labeled a Bible thumper—or worse—a Jesus freak.

As I waded slowly through the books of the Old Testament, I recognized a fair number of verses I had heard proclaimed in either my Protestant or Catholic worship experiences. However, there were many stories in the Bible that were completely foreign to me. There were stories that were surprising, sometimes shocking, at times even gruesome and bewildering. And there were women—lots of women—in the Bible. Some of them were the good kind of women you would expect from the pages of scripture. Others were downright scandalous. Some of their names were familiar to me, if only vaguely, but others were total strangers. A few of the stories caught my attention. These were stories of women who achieved important accomplishments, not by pretending to be men (as I had been doing at the office for so many years), but by doing and being quite the opposite—namely, by using their uniquely feminine attributes to achieve their desired ends.

For starters, there was Tamar from the book of Genesis. She was married to Judah's eldest son, Er. When Er died shortly after their wedding, Judah gave Tamar his next eldest son, Onan. This might sound odd to us, but it was Jewish custom to allow the widow to have offspring from her husband's bloodline. Onan, unfortunately, died shortly after the marriage. Judah next promised his youngest son, Shelah, to Tamar when that son would come of age, but Judah eventually reneged on this promise. No doubt he feared losing another son to this unlucky widow. Dejected, Tamar was determined to continue her first husband's bloodline and bring honor to his name. She cunningly disguised herself as a prostitute and lured Judah into having sex with her. When the unmarried Tamar was later discovered to be pregnant, Judah called for her death because she had dishonored his son. In response, Tamar produced Judah's signet ring, staff, and belt that she had taken as payment from him when she had been disguised as a prostitute. Judah was caught red-handed. He recognized his error and publicly declared Tamar's righteousness in fulfilling her widow's responsibility to see her husband's bloodline carried on. She gave birth to two sons, whom the people viewed as a double blessing from God. What's more, her firstborn son was an ancestor of David and, ultimately, Jesus Christ.

In Judges, I came across a wily woman named Jael who used her feminine charms to trap a dangerous enemy. The Israelites had been pursuing a Canaanite army led by a powerful commander named Sisera. In an attempt to escape, Sisera broke from his men and fled alone for safety. He eventually came to the tent of Jael. She recognized the enemy commander and offered him the hospitality of her tent. Once he was inside, she offered him a bottle of milk, which he gratefully accepted. Soon the great warrior fell asleep, and that's when Jael took action. She fetched a hammer and tent peg, and with one powerful blow, drove the peg through Sisera's head, thus achieving an important military victory for the Israelites.

In Samuel, I read about Abigail. She prepared a feast to settle a serious dispute between soon-to-be-king David and her rather arrogant husband, Nabal. Touched at her graciousness and sincerity, David agreed to pardon Nabal for his arrogance and spare Abigail's family. Nabal is said to have died from shock when he discovered his family could have been destroyed and that it was Abigail who had saved them. After the death of Nabal, David sent for Abigail to become his wife because of her virtue and her efforts to protect her family.

In the book bearing her name, I read about Ruth. She was the faithful daughter-in-law of Naomi. Ruth cared for Naomi when both of them became widowed, even though by Jewish law she was free to return to the home of her father. The situation of the women came to the attention of a kind and wealthy landowner, Boaz. He permitted Ruth to glean his fields for any scraps that might remain after the harvesting. Ruth's modesty, demeanor, devotion to family, and hard work captured the heart of Boaz, who honorably married her despite their different backgrounds. Among their offspring is Obed, father of Jesse and grandfather of David.

Then there was Esther, who also earned her own book in the Bible. She was married to King Ahasuerus of Persia, who did not know his wife was a Jew. When the king's right-hand man, Haman, conceived of a plan to kill the Jews, Esther got word of it. She could not go before the king without an invitation at the penalty of death. Instead, she rallied her people to fast for three days and nights, then prepared a special banquet for the king and Haman. Her charm and hospitality won the king's favor. When Esther told him of Haman's malicious plot, the king promptly sent him to the gallows.

These might not immediately sound like modern feminine heroes. Dressing like a prostitute to fool a father-in-law or driving a peg through someone's head are rather extreme actions. Nevertheless, I found something courageous, honorable, and just about these women. Tamar went to great lengths to honor the reputation of her deceased husband. Jael and Esther risked their lives to save their people. Abigail risked hers to rescue her family. Ruth desired to provide for her destitute mother-in-law, but only through an honorable marriage. All of these women called upon their God-given womanhood to make these outcomes happen, which both intrigued and challenged me.

As I continued working my way through the pages of scripture, I discovered plenty of women in the New Testament as well, including women who stood by Jesus until the bitter end, even when most of the men had scattered. Women were the first to be greeted by Christ at the Resurrection, and women became great disciples and witnesses to the faith. Above all, the greatest woman in the entire Bible was Mary, the mother of Jesus. She made God's plan for salvation possible, but not through royalty, education, wealth, or status. Mary accomplished it by freely offering the gift of herself. God had created her to be open to life, nurture and protect it, and bring it forth into the world—a world that would never be the same again. A man, simply by the nature of his biology, could not have performed this pivotal role in God's plan.

The women I encountered in God's holy book left me with thought-provoking concepts of what it means to be an authentic woman, and it opened my heart to wanting to learn more. I found additional answers in the deep wisdom of my first papal leader, the late Pope John Paul II.

John Paul II and the Dignity of Women

As I continued my studies of the Catholic faith into the 1990s, I noticed an interesting cultural shift underway. While feminism was surging, a simultaneous emasculation of men seemed to be taking place. It was best reflected in popular television sitcoms at the time such as *Murphy Brown*, *Roseanne*, *Frazier*, and *Married with Children*. In episode after episode, tough, bossy females bullied wimpy, clueless, and neurotic males (a formula that still seems to hold true in many TV programs today). Women who once struggled to be equal to men now seemed to be aggressively exchanging roles with them. The lines between femininity and masculinity were becoming blurred and "gender confusion" became a popular buzzword. Ironically, the individual whom God selected to help shed light on the tangled misperceptions of authentic masculinity and femininity was a single man who had never had sex at all.

Karol Wojtyla was a Polish Catholic whose mother died when he was only eight years old. Fortunately for Karol, his father was a strong male figure, firmly grounded in his faith. Karol learned at a young age to imitate that faith and embrace the Blessed Mother, his surrogate mother, in the core of his spirituality. As a young diocesan priest, Father Wojtyla surrounded himself with young couples, engaging them in deep and frank conversation about love and sexuality. He was fascinated with human relationships, and the insights he gained from his conversations and studies led to the publication of his first book, *Love and Responsibility*, which he authored as a bishop. It was candid and bold for a cleric in the 1950s to address such things as the importance of the female orgasm, and it revealed the counter-cultural thinking this man was capable of expressing. He continued his philosophical writing as cardinal and, more significantly, as Pope John Paul II, producing an impressive body of encyclicals, apostolic letters, books, and reflections.

The Holy Father was not a pope who remained hidden within the ivory towers of the Vatican. He was a man on the go, constantly intermingling with people young and old as he traversed the world with his message of hope. He embraced his people, instructed them, and listened to them. Perhaps due to his special relationship with the Virgin Mary, to whom he dedicated his pontificate with the words *totus tuus* ("totally yours"), this humble man in white seemed to have a special regard for women. He was well aware of how society was teaching women that their worth and dignity was based on things such as power, money, and control—particularly control of their own bodies. In answer to these deceptions, the Holy Father penned a 1988 apostolic letter, *Mulierus Dignitatum* (On the Dignity and Vocation of Women), which he later recapped in his 1995 *Letter to Women* for the occasion of the Fourth World Conference on Women, held in Beijing.

In these landmark writings, Pope John Paul II praised the unique gift of women to the Church and the world. He pointed out that men and women were both created in the image and likeness of God and that this important truth automatically granted them an equal dignity and vocation. Each gender had unique attributes and characteristics, but this was not to engage them in a battle of the sexes. On the contrary, males and females were designed to be perfectly complementary to one another. The Holy Father explained how men and women were called into a communion of loving human persons, not unlike the communion of Divine Persons in the Trinity. However, the perfect harmony and balance that God created in the days of Eden had been disrupted due to the fall of Adam and Eve and the introduction of original sin. This ushered in a reign of discord and contempt and male dominion: "Your desire shall be for your husband, and he shall rule over you" (Gn 3:16).

John Paul II positioned himself firmly as an advocate for women. He was quick to denounce the rampant discrimination against and exploitation of females throughout the world and argued for their equal opportunities in education, healthcare, and employment. He spoke out sharply against human trafficking. He also noted that feminine achievements were woefully missing from the annals of history and needed to be recognized. The pontiff praised women for their feminine genius, attributes, charisma, and holiness, and called upon them to employ these special gifts. He pointed out how women are an irreplaceable source of support and spiritual strength for others and how they can positively influence the various human communities they encounter.

The way for women to liberate themselves from male dominion, the pope cautioned, was not for women to take on male characteristics—as the world prescribed and as I had done for so many years in my office environments. Instead, the answer could be found only in women maintaining their own feminine originality. He called for women to make use of their innate ability to love the human beings God had entrusted to them. He praised them for their sensitivity and the importance they placed on relationships, and he said that the dignity of women was best witnessed in how they received love and gave it in return as a sincere gift of self. Finally, the Holy Father urged women everywhere to safeguard the moral dimensions of the culture and to be a powerful witness in the family, the Church, and the world.

In a way, John Paul was building upon what an earlier pope, Pius XI, wrote in his encyclical, *Casti Connubii* (On Christian Marriage): "For if the man is the head [of the family], the woman is the heart, and as he occupies the chief place in ruling, so she may and ought to claim for herself the chief place in love." This particular concept of womanhood was radically different from the ideology I had been taught in school and the professional world. I was beginning to understand that our equality as women came not from the things we could do, but from our inherent dignity and worth in being created in the image of God. Where we could really shine, what really sets us apart as a gender is that we—not men—hold the chief place in love. We are the heart, whether it is within the family, the social network, or the workplace. That influential power of love, I eventually discovered, would not only be transforming for me, but for those with whom I would come in contact.

Theology of the Body

Pope John Paul II made it a theme of his pontificate to expand upon the concept of sincere gift of self for all people—women and men—in order to become fully human and achieve true peace and happiness. He continued to explore authentic femininity and masculinity is a series of Wednesday audiences delivered between 1979 and 1984 that were eventually bundled into a theological masterpiece called *Theology of the Body*. It is a magnanimous work I'm only beginning to unpack—and will probably do so for the remainder of my life—because the riches are so profound.

Theology of the Body is an integrated vision of the human person—body, soul, and spirit—and a beautiful teaching of love, life, and human sexuality. Flying in the face of society's notions of these forces, the deep wisdom of *Theology of the*

Body is for people of all ages and vocations, inspiring us to live in a way worthy of our great dignity as human persons. It poignantly demonstrates that the union of the sexes proclaims and foreshadows the eternal union of Christ and the Church. George Weigel, in his bestseller *Witness to Hope: The Biography of Pope John Paul II*, calls *Theology of the Body* "one of the biggest reconfigurations of Catholic theology in centuries . . . a theological time-bomb set to go off with dramatic consequences . . . perhaps in the twenty-first century." The fuse is already burning. *Theology of the Body* is now being taught in a growing number of seminaries, schools, and parishes around the world. Its beauty and wisdom is beginning to resonate with non-Catholic audiences as well. At this rate, Pope John Paul II's inspired work may be our greatest hope for renewing marriage and family life in modern times.

Spiritual Companions

The strong women I met in the pages of scripture and the counter-cultural teaching of Pope John Paul II on authentic femininity were invaluable aids in helping me to recognize and appreciate myself as a woman. There was, however, another important factor in my journey that was equally beneficial—my introduction to the saints. Each holy soul I encountered seemed to offer a little nugget of wisdom that I could apply in my own life. There were three female saints in particular—Thérèse, Faustina, and Bernadette—who came into my life at particular times with a unique passion and purpose. The lessons of the way these women overcame the struggles of ordinary living with an extraordinary love for God has had a profound and lasting effect on me. Their virtuous example of faith, hope, and love continues to be a crucial help in my daily walk as woman, wife, and mother. To this very day, I consider them my special companions on the journey to holiness and joy, and I cannot imagine my spiritual life without their positive influence. I hope as I reveal them to you in the pages of this book, you will find them equally endearing.

VIRTUOUS COMPANIONS

I believe, as a woman, that having true female companions on our journey through life is a good thing. In fact, I think it essential. We may be blessed with adoring husbands, loving children, supportive parents, or loyal and friendly co-workers, but those relationships are never quite the same as having a close girlfriend or network of available female companions. Girlfriends fill a need for women that other people simply cannot fill. We can be ourselves with our girlfriends. We can dare to let down our guard, and for a few precious moments not worry about being supermom or superwife. We can laugh, talk about issues important to us, and feel loved, supported, and related to. Our girlfriends are there to celebrate the good times and walk with us through the bad. They provide more than just an emotional boost—they actually affect our physiological well-being. Scientific studies conducted by the UCLA

School of Medicine show that as women engage with one another, their bodies produce the hormone oxytocin, which is a natural stress reducer. Shelley E. Taylor, an internationally renowned scientist in the field of stress and health and a psychology professor at UCLA, later went on to write *The Tending Instinct: How Nurturing is Essential to Who We Are and How We Live* (Henry Holt). After conducting twenty-five years of research and analyzing 1,000 research studies, she concludes decisively in her book that women with strong female social ties are less prone to health risks and actually live longer than those who do not have these types of female friendships.

While growing up, I was fortunate to have three close girlfriends from elementary through high school. We were an inseparable group. Whether we were putting on skits, playing sports, or just hanging out, we enjoyed each other's company immensely. In college, I quickly became associated with another group of five girlfriends who filled my four years of higher learning with fun and fond memories.

Once I married, though, I chose to make my husband (and the four sons who would follow) the center of all my attention. I neglected to cultivate new close female relationships. I suppose that, at the time, I didn't think such friendships were necessary anymore. This was a real mistake. Don't get me wrong; I love being surrounded by the men in my family and being what my husband fondly refers to as "a rose among the thorns." I wouldn't trade it for the world, but I have also come to realize that a part of me mourns my lost network of girlfriends.

It's not that I haven't met women over the years that I'd like to be close friends with, but it just hasn't panned out for one reason or another. A few years ago, I was blessed to make a wonderful girlfriend who shared many of my primary interests (family, kids, and Catholic writing). All too quickly, however, I lost her to a horrific battle with cancer that left me aching and lonely. I had enormous difficulty getting over her death, although we had known each other only a relatively short time. It took the wisdom of a priest-friend who was my spiritual advisor to assist me in finally turning the corner in the grieving process. He helped me realize that my friend had represented female love to me, and that God had sent her to me as a special gift because I was lacking that kind of love in my life. His words brought light and healing to me. The hurt I was experiencing began to ebb, and I was eventually able to fully appreciate the gift—short as the time was—instead of only mourning the loss.

Friends in High Places

My friend's death has made me a bit cautious about looking for other close girlfriends. It's a self-protective mode of operation; I don't want to get hurt again, although I know that loss and separation are part of living and loving. I'm still working today on giving the whole girlfriend thing over to God and just being patient with it. I admit there have been times when I've wondered if God doesn't want me to get too distracted by relationships with others, since my vocation as wife, mother, and my various other ministries keep me plenty busy. But I quickly dismiss that idea. It's precisely in our relationships with others that we best experience God's love for us and best reflect that same love to others. God wants us to be people in relationship. He wants us to share our journeys with one another. I've learned invaluable lessons from the experiences of others, which I would never have discovered on my own, particularly in the area of spirituality. Interestingly, some of the greatest spiritual lessons and most intimate relationships with God I've been privy to share have come, not from people I've met in this life, but from some remarkable persons of faith that have gone before me. Specifically, I'm talking about the saints.

As a Catholic convert, I found the whole concept of a saint a new phenomenon. We never talked about saints in my particular branch of Lutheranism, nor did we refer to any particular individual by that title. To be honest, I wasn't particularly eager to learn about the saints at first. I thought they were going to be pretty boring people. I envisioned them as perfect Catholics from perfect families, praying all day and all night and never doing anything less than perfect. I could not have been more wrong. In the pages of saints' biographies, a whole new world opened to me. I discovered that saints were real people like us. Some were rather ordinary, while others were quite colorful. More than a few had interesting, even scandalous pasts. These were heroic figures from all walks of life and all parts of the world. They were men, women, and—I was surprised to learn—even children in some cases. Despite their different backgrounds—and, at times, quirky personalities—all of the saints had one thing in common: they were committed to knowing, loving, and serving God above all else.

The greatest treasure I eventually gleaned from the saints was far more than a good read. As I entered into their experiences, something was happening to me subconsciously. A subtle attraction toward these individuals was growing within me. I found myself wanting to be more like them. For the first time, I began to feel the desire in my soul: I wanted to be a saint. It wasn't for the earthly glory and fame (which isn't experienced in the saint's lifetime anyway, since sainthood isn't conferred until after a person dies). What attracted me was the idea of having such an awesome and intimate union with God, even when no one else knew about it—especially when no one else knew about it.

The more I studied, the more I began to understand that all of us are called to be saints in our own right. That's why the Church in its holy wisdom raised up (and continues to raise up) notable individuals as examples of holy living for us today in our own lives. This list of saints, of course, is not an all-inclusive one. I'm sure we all can think of deceased friends and relatives who were wonderful, caring people who are assuredly with God, but the Church knew we would benefit from a definitive collection of souls worthy of study and emulation.

What I found amazing in my study of the saints is the basis on which a person merits such a title. Since I'm a doer, I tend to judge my worth by how much I've accomplished and how well I'm producing. Similarly, I assumed saints earned their classification through great accomplishments such as having mystical visions or performing miracles. I was surprised to discover this was not the case at all. A Church-declared saint earns that title not by deeds but by heroic virtue. Saints become saints based on how they worked to overcome obstacles of all kinds, how they labored ceaselessly on their personality flaws, and how they tried to always keep their eyes on God. Like the rest of us, they were subject to things such as ridicule, persecution, illness, doubts, temptations, and sufferings of all kinds; but instead of succumbing, they became stronger and more focused to stay the course. Their example encourages us to pick ourselves up, try to choose the good, and keep our sights on the ultimate prize: God and heaven itself. The saints call us out of mediocrity, where the world would have us stay, and into greatness. They call us to be people of heroic virtue.

The Value of Virtue

Similar to sainthood itself, virtue was a new concept to me. I suppose I'd always had an understanding that, as human beings, we are called to be fundamentally good people and live decent lives. It was the Catechism of the Catholic Church, however, that gave me a better understanding of what virtue is and why it is important in our spiritual journey. To be virtuous, I learned, is to have a consistent and firm desire to do good, but virtue isn't limited to just performing worthy acts; it enables us to give the best of ourselves to those around us. It is our way of seeking and finding God and acting according to his will, instead of acting solely on the often-contradictory impulses of our own wills. Some virtues, I discovered, are infused into the souls of the faithful, while others are attainable through human effort, aided by grace. All of these positive traits or qualities need tender cultivation through things such as education, practice, and perseverance. Fortunately, God doesn't leave his children to stumble along. He gives us the grace to persevere in the pursuit of virtues if we continually ask for grace, frequent the sacraments, and cooperate with the Holy Spirit.

To guide us on our path to holiness, the Church identifies specific virtues worthy of our attention. For starters, there are the cardinal virtues, upon which all other virtues hinge (the word *cardinal* comes from the Latin word for "hinge"). The term was first coined by the famous ancient Greek philosophers, Plato and Aristotle, and the virtues were later adapted into Christianity by the early Church Fathers. The cardinal (sometimes called "moral") virtues are prudence (the ability to judge right from wrong), justice (the determination to see that someone is given his or her rightful due), fortitude (the strength to overcome fear and remain steadfast in the face of obstacles), and temperance (the restraint of our desires and passions to prevent excess and disorder).

In the Middle Ages, there was a focus on the subject of sin and temptation. Seven sins in particular were deemed "deadly" since they were viewed as the root of all other sin— pride, greed, gluttony, lust, sloth, envy, and anger. To counter the temptation to give in to these deadly vices, the Church produced a list of seven heavenly (or capital) virtues. They are humility (to be selfless and respectful of others), liberality (to give freely and generously without seeking recognition), chastity (to embrace wholesomeness and purity), meekness (to patiently seek resolution and to be merciful), temperance (to demonstrate self-control and moderation), kindness (to have compassion and charitable concern for others), and diligence (to be zealous in living and sharing the faith).

Faith, Hope, and Love

As I learned about the various virtues, it seemed reasonable to try to incorporate them into my life. After some initial practice, it became clear that they could be frustratingly elusive! But I came to see their value very quickly. The virtues I've found to have the most transformative effect—when I sincerely try to imitate them—are the three theological virtues: faith, hope, and love. These are the virtues that God infuses into our souls at Baptism, so maybe that's why they are so powerful. The theological virtues relate specifically to God and help us to live in a relationship with the Holy Trinity. They allow us to act as God's children and inherit eternal life. Sometimes the theological virtues are depicted by the symbol of a living tree in which faith is the root, hope is the trunk, and love is the fruit.

The theological virtues are intrinsically tied to one another. For example, the virtue of faith enables us to believe in God and all he has said and revealed. As disciples, we are called to keep the faith, live it, profess it, witness it, and spread it. Through faith, we commit our entire selves to God and seek to do only his will. A natural outcome of a lively virtue of faith is the desire and ability to produce good works.

The virtue of hope creates within us a desire for the kingdom of heaven and eternal life as our happiness. This virtue enables us to trust in Christ's promises for us. It allows us to rely on more than our own strength (which is inadequate), but on the help of the Holy Spirit. Hope inspires us and keeps us from discouragement. It sustains us during times of abandonment and preserves us from selfishness. Hope also affords us joy, even (and especially) in moments of great trial.

Love (also referred to as "charity") is the virtue by which we love God above all things for his own sake and our neighbor as ourselves for the love of God. St. Paul gives us one of the best definitions of this virtue when he writes:

> Love is patient and kind; love is not jealous or boastful; it is not arrogant or rude. Love does not insist on its own way; it is not irritable or resentful; it does not rejoice at wrong, but rejoices in the right. Love bears all things, believes all things, hopes all things, endures all things. (1 Cor 13:4–7)

While all three of the theological virtues are important, St. Paul tells us that love (or charity) is superior to the others. "So faith, hope, love abide, these three; but the greatest of these is love" (1 Cor 13:13 RSV). Since God is love and we are children of God, we are called to be people of love. We are not slaves acting in fear or workers performing for wages. We are God's children, operating in love. When we can remember to get out of the way and allow God's love to work through us, amazing things can happen. The great theologian St. Thomas Aquinas once made an interesting observation about love. He said, "To love is to will the good of another." This observation raises another powerful point about virtue. Virtue is not just about improving ourselves and enhancing our relationship with God; it is about the powerful effect virtue can have on others.

Virtue Is Contagious

As a woman, wife, and mother, I've seen the significant influence that virtue—and vice—can have on those around us. When I'm practicing vices or sins (which I'm afraid I do far too often), it always has negative repercussions on my husband, children, and anyone else who happens to be in my zone of fire. It seems to automatically draw out the worst in them. However, when through the grace of God I attempt to practice virtue, quite the opposite happens. It brings out the best in those around me. It may not happen immediately (especially if I've been over-practicing the vices!), but the transformation happens nonetheless.

If you are a single woman and desire to be married one day, the practice of virtue can really come in handy. I wish I had known this truth years ago, but I can see clearly today that virtue makes women attractive and desirable. It makes us beautiful inside and out. In fact, I've discovered it makes us irresistible. This is quite contrary to what the world professes. The world places no value on virtue. It is more apt to promote vice in the pursuit of capturing a man's attention. We see this by the popularity of immodest dress and behavior of many women today, particularly young women. Since virtue has been infused in the man's soul as well as ours, he instinctively recognizes it in a woman's heart and responds to it naturally. On a deep level, virtuous behavior draws him to want to please his beloved even more than he wants to please himself—ideally to the point of willingly laying down his life for her. A virtuous woman encourages self-giving love from the man rather than a self-centered lust. Whatever our state in life—single, married, or consecrated religious—virtue makes us most pleasing to God and is, therefore, desirable in its own right. Through it, we can teach others how to love.

When practiced well, there is simply nothing more powerful or influential than virtue.

Of course, none of us are perfect, and we will all fall short of living virtuous lives. We need to be patient and remind ourselves that we are each a work in progress. Becoming virtuous is a lifelong goal. The good news is, when we seek the virtues with earnest hearts through avenues such as the sacraments, Holy Mass, adoration, saints, and scripture, and when we protect ourselves from unbecoming images and entertainment, we discover that developing the habit of virtuous behavior becomes easier and more appealing. We can also seek shelter under the mantle of the greatest model of all virtue, Holy Mary. If we stick close to her and ask her intercession, she will most certainly come to our assistance.

My Special Spiritual Journey Partners

As we gain a better understanding of what virtues are and how transforming they can be to ourselves and others, it's easy to see why the Church uses virtue as her yardstick in measuring a person's sanctity. A saint's heroic virtue makes him or her worthy of our emulation. However, there is another inestimable benefit of learning about the saints and making them a part of our daily faith walk. It's simply this: saints are not static figures from history. They are not echoes from the past. Saints are alive and well and abiding in heaven. They have endured many of the trials we face in our own lives and want nothing more than to aid us in our spiritual journeys. More than just following their example, we can call on them—literally—to ask for their intercession as we bumble through our day-to-day existence. They are living helpers for us now, and all we need to do is to ask for their friendship and assistance. Not to make use of such an important resource and treasure is akin to trying to scale a steep mountain without the use of ropes, hardware, or a climbing partner. It's possible, but comes with far greater risk of slips and falls.

Each saint I've learned about has given me a little pearl of wisdom that has made me a better Catholic Christian; but, as I have mentioned, three in particular have graced my life in a special way and given me beautiful examples of the theological virtues of faith, hope, and love. As spiritual journey partners, Thérèse, Faustina, and Bernadette have changed my life forever. When I'm down and struggling, I can call on their assistance. While I can't get together with them for coffee in the morning or a martini after work, I know that these women hear me when I call. They understand and they encourage me. They aren't afraid to challenge me when I need it. Friends like these don't die, move away, or lose interest. They are in it for the long term, and that's a most consoling thought for the journey ahead.

A SHOWER
OF ROSES

My choice to convert to the Catholic faith in 1983 was not made on a whim. The seeds for such a fundamental decision had actually been planted early in my childhood. They were certainly not sowed there by my parents, who did not even like Catholics. They grew up in the Pelham and Van Nest sections of the Bronx in the 1930s and 1940s. While the New York metropolitan area was famously described as a "melting pot" in which immigrants of all backgrounds blended together into a harmonious common culture, this was not exactly my parents' experience. The way they described their childhood neighborhoods of bungalow homes and railroad-style houses, people tended to cluster together with their own kind. The Irish lived on one block, the Italians on another, and the Hispanics on still another. Catholics, Protestants, and Jews did not typically intermingle.

This segregated environment influenced my parents to be suspicious of anyone who looked, spoke, or worshipped differently; it was an attitude they never fully overcame. (They have both passed away now.) When they were adolescents, my father was an Episcopal altar server and my mother was a Lutheran Sunday-school teacher. They shared a common German heritage and in their twenties, were given permission by their parents to marry and move out to Long Island, where they raised five children in a small Cape Cod house with a real backyard on a cul-de-sac.

When they first moved out to Long Island, my parents found a local Lutheran community and became involved members. They adored the pastor, who baptized all five of us. In time, however, the pastor retired and a new pastor took his place. The new pastor was young and modern and had a completely different style from the former pastor, and my parents did not take well to him. Instead of finding another church—Lutheran or Episcopal—with a more agreeable pastor, they refrained from attending church at all. They saw to it that the five of us attended Sunday school and received Confirmation, but after that our religious destinies were up to us.

Although my siblings and I were baptized and confirmed Lutheran, it's more accurate to describe our upbringing as secular. Religion was not practiced or reinforced in our home in any way that I can remember. Rather we were outsourced to Sunday school to receive religious education. We did not speak of God or pray to him as a family. There was nothing on the walls of our home to indicate we were Christians of any sort. Christmas was centered on presents and Santa Claus, and Easter was all about the Easter Bunny and hunting for eggs. Jesus was simply not a part of our holiday celebrations.

Despite this secular family environment, I had an experience with faith that was very different from that of my siblings. From a very young age, I felt supernaturally led by a God who was far more real to me than the one talked about in my Sunday-school lessons. I believed with all my heart that this God knew me, loved me, and wanted to be an intimate and active part of my life. This was not something I learned from my parents; it was something much more profound than the simple Sunday-school lyrics we used to sing: "Jesus loves me, this I know. For the Bible tells me so." It was more of an instinctual, inherent knowing that I can only surmise was granted through the grace of God. This is not to say I was some saintly, extraordinary kid who deserved special knowledge or privileges; far from it. On the outside, I was no different from any other child. I did my fair share of bending the truth, fighting with siblings, and disobeying my parents. On many nights, however, in the privacy of my shared bedroom, I spoke silently to this personal God in my heart. I sent my long list of "please give mes" into the dark, hoping my wishes would all be granted. Before closing my eyes for the night, I also remembered to end my supplications by telling this God that I loved him. Regardless of whether or not I received whatever I happened to be asking for, I trusted that God was somewhere out there listening. Once when I was eight, I believe this God actually responded to me. It was a short but powerful promise whispered into my heart: "I have a special mission for you." He didn't specify at the time what that mission was, but these words would remain permanently etched in my soul. It was like a secret Nancy Drew mystery that only I could solve. I had a mission. God had plans for my life.

Catholic Clues

Most of my friends and neighbors growing up were Catholic. It was okay to have them as friends, but I wasn't allowed to go to church with them or attend their prayer groups. My

parents passed along to their children typical myths about
Catholicism, such as how Catholics worshipped Mary and
how they were trying to take over the world by having such
large families. My parents didn't single out the Catholic
Church; they were equal-opportunity discriminators as a
result of their Bronx upbringing. They did have a particular
beef with the Church, though, stemming from an incident
that happened early in their married life. When their close
friend was preparing to marry a Catholic girl, he wanted my
parents to be the best man and maid of honor. This wasn't
permitted because neither of my parents were Catholic. My
parents didn't understand that in the Catholic Church, the
best man and maid of honor are important witnesses to a
sacrament and, as such, are responsible for supporting the
couple in their faith walk. The message my parents took away
from this situation was that they weren't good enough for the
Catholic Church, and that message left a lasting hurt.

I wasn't privy to all of that background as a child, but
I did learn pretty quickly that Catholics were different from
us and we needed to watch out for them. I can remember
my Catholic neighbors celebrating strange rituals involving little white dresses or black smudges on their foreheads.
My parents preferred to keep their distance, but I found the
whole Catholic thing mysterious and intriguing. Looking
back, I think my curiosity about Catholicism was encour-
aged to some degree by some of the entertainment of the
1960s. For example, I have vivid memories of trying to sing
along with a 45 rpm of "Dominique," the international hit by
the Belgian Dominican Sister Jeanine Deckers, dubbed "The
Singing Nun." I remember packing into the family station
wagon to see *The Sound of Music* at the local drive-in, where
we were charmed and captivated by nun-in-training Maria
(Julie Andrews). We rarely missed an episode of *The Flying
Nun*, enjoying the latest antics of Sister Bertrille (Sally Fields),

who could even take to the air due to her small stature and heavily starched cornette. Somehow as long as the nuns were singing, dancing, or flying, they were okay with my parents.

In my hometown, an order of real-life nuns called the Sisters of Mercy ran an orphanage for boys. In those days, the Sisters of Mercy wore traditional black-and-white habits with a large rosary hanging from their side. Our family would drive past their convent routinely on the way to my grandparents' house. Each time, I would peek out of the back of the station-wagon window, eager to catch a glimpse of one of the sisters walking the grounds with her long veil flowing in the wind. Once, quite innocently, I announced to my family that one day I might like to become a nun. That did not go over too well. In fact, I'm surprised my mother didn't lose control of the steering wheel; she certainly lost control of her temper. She ranted over how I could make such a ridiculous statement when we weren't even Catholic. Surprised at her sudden vehemence, I decided it was probably better to keep such things to myself.

The Medal

There was another important Catholic "clue" I discovered in second grade that stopped me in my tracks. Walking the familiar route to my neighborhood public elementary school, I noticed something shiny and silver lying on the sidewalk. I picked it up and studied it closely and realized I had found a Catholic religious medal. I knew this because I had a number of Catholic friends making their First Holy Communion at the time, and medals such as these were common gifts. On the front of the medal was a woman wearing a veil and holding a cross and flowers in her arms. I assumed the smiling lady must be Mary, because I didn't know at eight years old that Catholic medals could depict anyone else. (After all, didn't Catholics worship her?) On the back of the medal was the cryptic inscription, "After my death I shall let fall a shower of roses." These words were as strange to me as Egyptian hieroglyphics. I knew they meant something, but I had no idea what. I could not recall from my Sunday school classes any stories of the Virgin Mary and flowers falling from the sky. Truthfully, I think the reason I decided to put the medal in my pocket that day had less to do with the mysterious words on the back and more to do with the tiny little stones in the front—stones that seemed to almost wink at me. I thought perhaps I had found valuable jewels.

After school that day, I showed the medal to my mother. I pointed out the little stones and asked if they were real. She studied the object for a moment and handed it back to me, uninterested. "No," she responded. "I doubt it's very valuable. But you can keep it if you want." And with that she went about her business. This was probably my mother's way of saying I didn't have to try to track down the owner of the medal to return it, but to me this was nothing short of a true miracle. I think I stood there for several moments with my mouth open. I could keep this? But wasn't it—Catholic? I decided not to give my mother a chance to reconsider her decision, but scurried off to put this forbidden little treasure in my jewelry box. Little did I know I had just met my first spiritual journey partner.

Falling Away

Sunday school at my Lutheran church was not something I particularly enjoyed. To be honest, I found the whole thing rather boring. I cannot, to this day, remember much of what I was taught or who taught it to me—with the exception of one teacher I had in the seventh grade. She loved to divert from the workbook to tell us fascinating stories of how the world was going to end in the mid-1980s. It really made the hour go by fast. Then one of my classmates mentioned the unorthodox curriculum to her father and soon after we had a new seventh-grade teacher, and it was back to the same old workbook.

Once I reached ninth grade and preparation for my Lutheran Confirmation, we were required to attend Sunday school and worship in the big church upstairs. This was even less appealing to me than Sunday school because I had to sit all by myself in the sanctuary. My parents were no longer going to church, my older brother and sister had stopped going immediately after they were confirmed, and my two younger sisters were still in Sunday school and too small for the big church. As I sat there alone in the pew, I found it hard to pay attention. Every Sunday-school teacher had told us that this was God's house (I think it was their way of getting us to behave properly), but I did not experience God there—not in the pastor's sermons or the monthly Communion service or the big empty cross at the front wall of the sanctuary. For me, God dwelled in one place: in my heart, in the privacy of my bedroom.

As Confirmation time drew closer, I found myself looking forward to the event. I knew I would get a new dress and a party with presents. I also knew that once Confirmation was over, I no longer had to attend Sunday school or worship in the big church. At last I would be a free agent! As a part of the festivities, I was chosen by my classmates to create the cover for our Confirmation program. My design was pretty simple. I wrote "Confirmation" in Old English lettering across the bottom. That gave it a good Lutheran feel. Above these words I drew a crown, as we were always talking about priest, prophet, and king. Above that, I drew three birds in the shape of doves hovering over it all, sort of like the Father, Son, and Holy Spirit. The teacher commended me on my drawing and it became the cover for the program.

What I find interesting today as a Catholic convert is that no one questioned me back then about the doves. I didn't know it at the time, but in the Lutheran faith, Confirmation is not considered a sacrament. It is seen more as a rite of passage as the young man or woman partaking in this ritual becomes an adult member of the church. There is no conferring of grace. There is no Holy Spirit. Somehow I got things a bit mixed up. In my mind, I was sure something special was going to happen at my Confirmation. I even felt it the moment my parents, my godparents, and my pastor placed their hands on my head. I experienced a tangible sense of empowerment, a strong surging through my body. Perhaps I was feeling the power of being prayed over, which can be powerful no matter what faith you happen to be. Or maybe it was some kind of foreshadowing of my future Catholic Confirmation.

In any event, once Confirmation was over and all that was left was the big church and a youth group that wasn't particularly exciting, I executed my right to sleep in on Sundays. My personal God, the one I used to talk to nightly, was put on a back burner as I began to immerse myself in sports and other high-school activities. I rarely talked to him unless I needed help with a test or some other important favor. For the most part, like so many other teens and young adults, I fell away into secularism.

College Days

God was still on the back burner, not even at a simmer, when I left for college at the University of Bridgeport in Connecticut. I can remember on one of the first days of school a female minister coming into the cafeteria wearing a smile that was a little too big for her face. She was handing out flyers inviting all of the Protestant students to join her each Sunday on a bus that would take them to various churches to worship. There were two problems with her invitation. First, I had never encountered a female minister before and was a bit put off by her forwardness. Second, and more importantly, I had no desire to go to different churches in downtown Bridgeport to worship. If you are familiar with various Protestant expressions of worship, you may know that they are very different from one another. The Baptists are not like the Presbyterians. The Evangelicals are different from the Methodists. It's not like going to the Catholic parish across town, across the country, or even across the world, where the Mass is the same fundamental experience. It can be more like going to church on another planet. I accepted the woman's flyer with a polite smile and pitched it in the trash on the way out of the cafeteria.

Two years later, I think God got had gotten tired of being on that back burner. To shake things up a bit, he sent into my life a young man, Mark, who eventually became my husband. Mark was Catholic and Italian, and I wondered just how well that was going to go over with my parents. He was not overt about his Catholic faith, nor did he act any differently from all the other college students—except for one thing. Almost every Sunday evening, I noticed that Mark went over to the little Newman Center across from our dormitories for Mass. I was pretty impressed with that, because no one was forcing him to go; he just went. One evening Mark invited me to go to the Newman Center with him. The forbidden mystery of the Mass was finally being offered to me, which sparked my curiosity. I figured my parents would never have to know about it, so I agreed.

There were several things that struck me about that first Mass experience. For starters, it was a very simple setting with only about a dozen or so students in attendance. The atmosphere was quite casual. Kids were dressed in sweats and jeans, and the priest had long hair and wore sandals.

I remember being distracted all through the Mass because I had never seen a minister's toes before. The songs were folksy with a guitar player providing music. There was no organ or pomp and circumstance like in the Lutheran church, but there was something else. Despite the lack of formality, there was a palpable sense of community in this small worship space. I suspect it wasn't because the kids knew each other. They had come from all over the campus, and UB was a pretty big school. Yet the Mass seemed to somehow create unity among them. It was like they were all a part of a club of which I wasn't a member.

The most memorable part of that first Mass, however, was the moment when the priest held that little white wafer above his head and said the words of consecration. Suddenly I knew. I recognized it was Jesus Christ in that Eucharist. No one had to explain it to me with deep theological arguments. I just recognized him. I can even remember thinking, "Oh, so that's where you've been hiding!" Like the eyes of the disciples when they were walking on the road to Emmaus, my own eyes were opened that day in the breaking of the bread. My eyes were opened to the fact that the one who stood before me was truly Jesus. This was a true turning point for me, because up until that moment, God had never manifested himself to me in a public setting. Now I understood that God could exist in public worship and not just in the depths of my heart. The fact that it had taken place in a Catholic Mass, however, was more than a bit troublesome to me.

As time went on, I began falling more in love with Mark and more in love with the Catholic Mass. Still, I was resistant to the idea of actually becoming Catholic. Mark and I were beginning to talk of marriage, so I proposed a compromise. Perhaps, I suggested, we could find another faith we could make our own. Mind you, I wasn't suggesting Buddhism or Islam; I was intending on staying within the Christian realm.

Mark wasn't particularly interested in a compromise, and that's when I began to realize how deep his roots were in his Catholic faith. During a semester break in my senior year, I returned home and made an appointment with the associate pastor of my Lutheran church to discuss some questions I was having. In that meeting, I asked about where our church stood on specific issues like abortion or contraception, which I knew were important in the Catholic faith. His answers were rather non-committal. I kept pressing him and contrasting his answers with what the Catholic Church taught. He could see pretty quickly where I was headed, so finally he said, "The way I see it, the Catholic Church is a church with a lot of rules. If you're a person who needs a lot of rules in your life, maybe that's the one for you." I left the meeting feeling puzzled and dissatisfied. Okay, so the Church had rules. What was wrong with that? Wasn't it important to have concrete truths and realities and for believers to believe the same thing? I had no desire to belong to a wishy-washy faith. These intellectual thoughts made it safe for me to consider breaking away from the church of my youth, but what was far more compelling was the surge of emotion rising inside of me. I knew in my heart of hearts that I wanted to share the same faith with my future husband. I didn't want to raise our children in a split-faith environment and force them to choose. Most of all, I wanted to be a part of a worship environment where I experienced the true presence of God—the real and personal God whom I had loved so dearly in my childhood. Every sign was pointing to the Roman Catholic Church.

Catholic Neophyte

A year after graduation, I signed up for religious-instruction classes in New York at St. Patrick's Cathedral, which was a block away from my city advertising job. I attended these classes during my lunch hour with a small group of adults and a priest whose job it was to try to teach us the fundamentals of the Catholic faith. Later that summer, I took the plunge. I became Catholic in a small and simple ceremony with the same priest presiding. The Mass was held in the back chapel of St. Patrick's on a warm Saturday morning while tourists walked around and admired the side altars and stained-glass windows of the impressive cathedral. Mark, who had become my fiancé, was my sponsor. I anticipated thunderbolts and lightning for such a momentous decision, but the liturgy was a calm and quiet event, even at the moments of Confirmation and receiving Eucharist. My life as a Catholic neophyte had begun.

Mark's entire family was in attendance for the celebration, but no one from my family was; I hadn't told them about my decision. I was planning to, eventually, but I judged they wouldn't understand such a radical decision. More to the point, I feared they might present objections or cause a scene. I decided to let my parents in on my conversion after the fact, and as I suspected, they didn't understand it. But I was twenty-three, engaged, and, after all, they had put my religious destiny in my own hands. Entering the Catholic Church was a definite stepping away from my biological family—one that still creates a bit of separation because it is such an enormous part of my life that my family doesn't share. It's not that they've ostracized me or have ever tried to discourage me, but it does make me different. When I hear the scriptural verses that talk about Jesus coming not to unite but to divide, it hits me in a poignant way:

> Do you think that I have come to give peace on earth? No, I tell you, but rather division; for henceforth in one house there will be five divided, three against two and two against three; they will be divided, father against son and

son against father, mother against daughter and daughter
against her mother, mother-in-law against her daughter-
in-law and daughter-in-law against her mother-in-law.
(Lk 12: 51–53)

Fortunately God is generous and he rewards our sacrifices. In making the conscious decision to follow Jesus more
closely, I have not lost my family. Rather, I have become a part
of an even larger one—the Catholic Church.

Identifying the Medal

Once I had become a Catholic, I realized it was time for me
to understand exactly what I had gotten myself into. Like
many converts, I had been led on the early stages of my spiritual journey primarily by my heart and my emotions, but
now the time had come for me to dive in and really understand the teachings of this immense Church I had just joined.
To expand upon what I had learned in my RCIA classes, I
began an intense study of Catholicism, which included my
introduction to the lives of the saints. It was when studying
these remarkable men and women that I was finally able to
identify correctly the image on the medal I had found as a
child—the medal I still kept tucked in my jewelry box. To my
great surprise, the woman on the medal was not the Virgin
Mary at all. The mysterious words, "After my death I shall
let fall a shower of roses," were actually spoken by a young
French nun named St. Thérèse of Lisieux, nicknamed the
"Little Flower."

I remember feeling a little disconcerted at the thought
of a total stranger residing in my jewelry box for the past
fifteen years. Granted, I had never worn the medal, but it
was a strange feeling just the same. I began to wonder who
this woman was and if there was a reason for my having
kept the medal all those years. I decided the least I could do

was to get to know St. Thérèse better. I picked up a copy of her autobiography, *Story of a Soul,* and like the millions who have been privileged to read this precious glimpse into the life of a great saint, I fell head over heels in love with her. Our souls connected. I became firmly convinced that finding the medal when I was eight years old was not happenstance. It was meant to be. Thérèse had been sent into my life in my childhood to watch over me and guide me, like a guardian angel, even when I didn't know who she was or why our paths had crossed. Somehow I knew this nun, who was born a century before me in a land an ocean away, was meant to play a special part in my life, and indeed she would. St. Thérèse became a central figure in the start of my writing ministry and the saint who best taught me how to love. But before I share that story, I'd like to tell you hers.

Thérèse:
Master of Love

Marie-Françoise-Thérèse Martin entered the world on January 2, 1873, at a time when French Catholicism was extremely rigid and set squarely against the nation's growing secularism. Although the Church declared the movement heresy, many of the faithful in Thérèse's time were still deeply influenced by a seventeenth-century ideology known as Jansenism. Jansenism held a pessimistic view of humanity that over-emphasized the effects of original sin. It asserted that people are basically incapable of good and that only a certain portion of humanity is predestined to be saved. God is viewed primarily as a god of justice, one that had to be appeased by good works and a strict aversion to sin. One of the greatest errors of Jansenism was that it denied the role of a person's free will in the acceptance and use of God's grace.

God used Thérèse to teach the world a radically different viewpoint: that the grace he gave so freely was an open invitation to holiness and love that by its nature elicited a free response. God was a god of love and mercy, and this liberating message took the world by storm.

Family Life

Thérèse's parents, Louis and Zélie Martin, were devout Catholics who were well aware of the rising influence of secularism and the persecution of the Church in parts of France. Like many Catholic middle-class families, they tended to separate themselves from sinful worldly influences and keep to themselves and their religious traditions. In those days, the role of priest and nun were considered more spiritually elevated than the vocation of marriage, so it is not surprising that both of Thérèse's parents had been initially attracted to religious life. Louis became a watchmaker after he was refused entrance to the monastery of St. Bernard for not knowing Latin. He settled in Alençon, a town one hundred miles west of Paris, which was famous for its lacemaking. There he met and married young Zélie Guerin, who also had been unable to fulfill her aspirations for religious life and who had instead become a fine lacemaker. When they were first married, the couple lived together as brother and sister until a priest discouraged them from doing that. Obediently they began their family of nine children, of which only five daughters survived: Marie, Pauline, Léonie, Céline, and Thérèse, the youngest.

Although the Martins were reasonably well-off as members of the business class, Louis and Zélie demonstrated a firm detachment from worldly things. Eternal life was their dominant concern, and the couple made it a point to shelter their daughters from harmful influences. They were a close-knit group, centered on God and their Catholic faith. Daily

Mass, family prayer, almsgiving, and serving others were a way of life for the family. Using family letters as evidence, Thérèse later described herself as a precocious child, a bit impish, and stubborn. She could be extremely touchy and subject to sudden outbursts of temper. She had an attraction to good at an early age, but was not always successful in achieving it. Her greatest character flaw, she claimed, was that she had "excessive self-love." Rooting out this sin became a lifelong struggle for her.

This self-love was different from the love that her parents and older sisters freely showered upon Thérèse, and she readily recognized the difference. "All my life God was pleased to surround me with love . . . and the first memories I have are stamped with smiles and the most tender caresses." Louis Martin fondly referred to his youngest daughter as his "Little Queen" and did not hide his particular affection for her, yet he was careful not to spoil her in terms of behavior. He did not permit a fault to go unnoticed, but corrected Thérèse with charity. From the time she was a small child, Thérèse had an attraction to God and a desire to please him. She liked to go off by herself and think about God and heaven, and it was obvious to others that she was receiving tremendous graces and wisdom through this unusual contemplation.

One of her favorite places to contemplate God was among the gardens and flowers. She felt close to her Creator there and learned important lessons from nature that would influence her life and spirituality:

> I understood how all the flowers he has created are beautiful, how the splendor of the rose and the whiteness of the lily do not take away the perfume of the little violet or the delightful simplicity of the daisy. I understood that if all flowers wanted to be roses, nature would lose her springtime beauty, and the fields would no longer be decked out with little wild flowers. And so it is in the world of souls,

Jesus' garden. He willed to create great souls comparable to lilies and roses, but he has created smaller ones and these must be content to be daisies or violets destined to give joy to God's glances when he looks down at his feet. (*Story of a Soul*, 14)

Thérèse happily saw herself as the littlest of flowers in God's garden, and this is a metaphor that eventually played an important part of her spirituality.

The Challenges Begin

When Thérèse was four, her mother died, darkening Thérèse's happy life. This devastating loss caused her to become timid, withdrawn, self-protective, and more sensitive than ever. Her only happiness was in the security of her family circle. For this reason, Louis relocated his family to Lisieux to be closer to his wife's relatives. In the absence of Zélie Martin, Thérèse chose her older sister, Pauline, to become her "mother." She and Pauline had always been close and shared the same deep love and desire for God. Pauline tutored Thérèse and followed her father's example by being careful not to spoil her little sister. When correction was required, Thérèse accepted it without excuse and seemed to learn quickly from her mistakes. Pauline also taught her younger sibling how to make little voluntary sacrifices for the conversion of sinners and even gave her a little string of beads on which she could count her good deeds and sacrifices.

At eight years of age, Thérèse began attending a Benedictine school, but this was a miserable experience for her. Since she was so well prepared academically by Pauline, she was put into a class of children thirteen and fourteen years of age, but her academic success at school only drew the scorn of her jealous classmates. Thérèse could not relate to her classmates, who had little concern for God but great interest in worldly affairs. She bore all of this without complaint, but for her it was like a martyrdom of body and soul. She suffered increasing headaches and extreme sensitiveness of heart. She cried frequently over the least bit of trouble and then cried again for having cried.

A year later, Thérèse suffered another crushing loss when Pauline decided to enter the Carmelite convent in Lisieux. Thérèse desperately wanted to go with her, but she was only nine and one had to be sixteen to be accepted into the order. Even the weekly visits to see Pauline in the parlors at the convent did not assuage the heartbreak. Soon the youngest Martin became sick with a mysterious illness that baffled her family and doctors. For six months, Thérèse suffered tremors, sweating, and strange hallucinations. Her visions were so horrifying that people began to wonder if the devil had something to do with it. At times she tried (and sometimes succeeded) to fling herself off her bed. Other times she would screech with her face contorting in pain, and her family feared she would die. Louis, in desperation, had a novena of Masses said at Our Lady of Victories in Paris. At the end of that novena, while Marie, Léonie, and Céline were praying fervently before a statue of the Blessed Mother at the bedside of their stricken sister, a miracle occurred. Thérèse stared at the statue and suddenly grew calm and even smiled. She reported later that the statue had disappeared and was replaced by the real Virgin Mary, looking radiant with a beautiful smile. The illness left her and Thérèse was cured.

With Pauline lost to her at Carmel, Thérèse was next put in the charge of her eldest sister, Marie. Marie taught her little pupil all about virtue, which immediately attracted Thérèse as a viable means of loving God and attaining heaven, especially if carried out in a hidden way:

> Soon God made me feel that true glory is that which will last eternally and to reach it, it isn't necessary to perform

striking works but to hide oneself and practice virtue in such a way that the left hand knows not what the right hand is doing. (*Story of a Soul,* 72)

It was during this period that Thérèse began immersing herself in books about the saints. She was particularly drawn to the life of Blessed Joan of Arc (who was canonized after Thérèse's lifetime). Thérèse had the feeling she was born for glory but not glory that would be evident in the eyes of mortals. She believed her glory would consist in becoming a great saint. She knew full well she was weak and imperfect and incapable of doing this on her own. But she resolved:

I don't count on my merits since I have none, but I trust in him who is virtue and holiness. God alone, content with my weak efforts, will raise me to himself and make me a saint, clothing me with his infinite merits. (*Story of a Soul,* 72)

At the age of eleven, Thérèse began preparing for her First Holy Communion, although in her heart she had been anticipating this special day for years. This was the day she would give herself totally to Jesus. She had sat in on Marie's preparation of Céline for her First Holy Communion two years earlier, and Thérèse had decided secretly to prepare herself by giving Jesus a bouquet of sacrifices every day. She made a powerful retreat a few days before her First Holy Communion and wrote the following resolutions: (1) I will never allow myself to be discouraged, (2) I will say the Memorare every day, and (3) I will try to humiliate my pride. On the day she received the Eucharist for the first time, which she referred to as her first kiss from Jesus, she felt united to him for life. The occasion was extra sweet because Pauline was making her profession of vows at the Carmelite monastery the very same day. A month later, Thérèse was confirmed according to custom and even further propelled in her love for God. Receiving Jesus in the Eucharist was such a transforming experience for the young child that she begged the priest to receive the Eucharist more often than once a week and was granted the exceptional permission to receive on feast days.

Struggles and Victories

In the next two years, Thérèse worked diligently on practicing virtue and developing a humble patience for whatever suffering might come her way. Inwardly she felt that God and the Holy Virgin had preserved her from the seduction of the world and she must always be mindful of this. At the same time, she developed a serious bout of scruples and became borderline-neurotic over every slightest fault in herself. She grew more sensitive than ever. To add to her suffering, Thérèse had to bid farewell to Marie as she entered Carmel, and to Léonie as she left to join the Poor Clares. (Léonie eventually left this order and found her true vocation as a Visitation sister in the monastery at Caen after a few false starts.) The Martin family was reduced to Céline and Thérèse, the two youngest Martin girls, who lived with and cared for their aging father, Louis.

At Christmas that year, Thérèse experienced a tremendous grace from God that would enable her to finally overcome her scrupulosity and oversensitivity. She described this event as her "conversion." As she, Céline, and her father were returning from Midnight Mass, she overheard a tired Louis commenting to Céline that he was glad that this would be the last year of the childish tradition of placing gifts in the shoes, since Thérèse was getting too old for such things. Normally a situation like this would have caused young Thérèse to dissolve into tears. Instead, she went to her bedroom and prayed before her crucifix and discovered in doing so an inner strength she seemed to have lost at the age of four when her mother died. Thérèse felt herself become a new person on what she would refer to later as this "night of light."

This experience turned Thérèse's attention outward in a powerful way. She soon developed a strong desire to work for the conversion of sinners. "I felt a charity enter into my soul, and the need to forget myself and to please others; since then I've been so happy!" Contemplating Jesus on the cross, Thérèse was inspired spiritually to catch the precious drops of blood that fell from his hands and pour them out among souls. Jesus' words from the cross, "I thirst," ignited within her a living fire. She developed a burning desire to save souls to console Jesus and quench his thirst. Souls of great sinners held the greatest attraction. Her first experiment was a convicted criminal named Henri Pranzini, a man who had been sentenced to death for the murder of three people. Thérèse prayed unceasingly for his repentance. Right before his execution, Pranzini surprised the attending priest by asking for the crucifix and kissing it lovingly. Thérèse considered this repentant criminal her "first child," and would make saving souls one of her life's ambitions.

Desire for Religious Life

Thérèse's thirst for the souls of sinners continued to grow as her love for Jesus grew. She still found practicing virtue to be hard, but it was becoming more sweet and natural to her. Hungry for spiritual knowledge, she found it now in only two sources: holy scripture and The Imitation of Christ, which she had memorized by heart.

For as long as she could remember, Thérèse wanted to be a religious. As each of her three older sisters left for religious life, she felt more distraught at still being in the world and not at Carmel. To find peace, she turned in prayer to the children her mother had lost in childbirth, whom she called the "four angels." She asked for their intercession, and it seemed to help. Calling upon her heavenly siblings became a practice she used often in times of need.

Initially, Thérèse was attracted to the idea being a hermit so she could truly be alone with God. She also thought of doing mission work in faraway places. Finally, she decided that to enclose herself in Carmel and remain hidden forever would be the greater sacrifice and would win more souls for Jesus.

Thérèse confided her desire to enter Carmel to her sole remaining sister, Céline, who revealed a similar calling. Even though Céline was older, she recognized that God was calling Thérèse first, and she willingly made the sacrifice to stay and care for their father. Thérèse chose Pentecost to tell Louis about her desire to enter Carmel the following year at the age of fifteen, and although he shed tears at the prospect of losing his Little Queen, he too recognized his daughter's calling. Desire alone was not enough to enter Carmel, however. There were obstacles. The ecclesiastical superior of the Lisieux Carmel, Father Delatroëtte, felt it was imprudent to admit Thérèse before the age of twenty-one. Though she was heartbroken at the news, Thérèse did not give up. She and her father arranged a meeting with their bishop to take up the matter. Thérèse even put her hair up for the meeting so she would appear older. The bishop was both touched and amazed to see a father and daughter so passionate about the same unusual cause. He promised he would ask the superior about it, but that did not comfort Thérèse. She knew the superior was firm in his decision.

There was, however, one last hope for Thérèse. Her diocese had planned a pilgrimage to Rome to celebrate the Jubilee year instituted by Pope Leo XIII. Louis, Céline, and Thérèse were scheduled to go. Thérèse decided to take her cause before the highest authority on earth. Even though it was forbidden to speak to the pontiff at the time of blessing,

Thérèse summoned the courage to speak boldly and defend her vocation: "Holy Father, in honor of your jubilee, permit me to enter Carmel at the age of fifteen!" Pope Leo XIII was stunned at this request but also impressed at the child's conviction. His answer, though, was not what she had hoped to hear: "Do what the superiors tell you. You will enter if God wills it." A dejected Thérèse returned to Lisieux thinking she had failed in her mission. She had done everything in her power; now the matter was in God's hands. On New Year's Day, her prayers were answered in a letter from the Mother Superior at Carmel indicating that the bishop had approved her entrance to Carmel. To appease those who had been opposed to the idea, her entrance was delayed until after Lent. Three months seemed forever to Thérèse, but she used the time of waiting to do penances and mortifications and work on breaking her self-will. On April 9, 1888, her religious aspirations were finally achieved as she formally entered the Carmelite convent in Lisieux.

Carmel at Last

Thérèse had entered Carmel, in her own words, to save souls and pray especially for priests. Jesus helped the young nun understand that this task would be best accomplished through her willing acts of sacrifice and suffering. Most of her suffering as a religious was internal and unknown to the community of two-dozen sisters. On the outside, her simplicity and humility made her pass practically unnoticed among much of the community. There were those who were jealous that the mother superior had bent the rules to enable three Martin sisters to live in the same community, but Thérèse showed no partiality toward her biological sisters. She had come to give her life to God. The newest Carmelite quickly demonstrated a respectful detachment from Pauline and Marie and made it her practice to love all the sisters in her community equally, even (and especially) the more difficult ones. It was these challenging sisters she patiently tolerated and whose company she sought at recreation.

Those nuns who were privileged to observe Thérèse more closely were amazed by her virtue. Even the older nuns often sought her counsel. They watched as Thérèse faithfully and generously practiced the mortifications prescribed by the rule of her order. What they didn't know was that the young nun would have liked to increase those penances, but she was not permitted to do so because of her frail health. Thérèse accepted the lowliest jobs cheerfully and did them to the best of her ability. Without complaint, she ate whatever was served to her, even if it disagreed with her. By her joyful disposition, one would assume that sacrifices and virtue came easy to the little nun, but in truth it was a daily struggle due to her strong temperament.

Inside the walls of the cloister, Thérèse flourished, growing both in grace and wisdom. She received many lights in prayer and seemed to unlock the rich secrets of scripture, which she shared with the other sisters in advising them. Jesus' words were so important to her that she carried copies of the gospels close to her heart. One of her responsibilities at the convent was to look after the novices, although she was never given the title of novice mistress. Still she taught the young girls with great wisdom and good sense. She was not afraid to be disliked by these young girls; her prime concern was the sanctity of each novice. Many were difficult to work with, but Thérèse handled each one as necessary, knowing how to urge souls toward virtue at their own pace. As her father had done with her, she told the novices their faults firmly but charitably.

Inwardly Thérèse strove courageously for perfection, both in great trials and in the minutiae of religious practices. Her daily goal was to embrace every opportunity to make some small sacrifice, control every look and every word, and profit by doing even the least actions with great love. Her desire was to be unknown, forgotten, and counted as nothing.

Trials

The suffering that Jesus promised Thérèse as the price for saving souls was never lacking. The clash of personality styles within the community and the constant and unmerited public scoldings she received from her mother superior, who was determined not to spoil the child, were only the beginning of the challenges she faced. A great trial for the young Carmelite was the demise and death of her beloved father. Paralysis had taken over his body and his brain until he eventually had to be sent to a mental home. People gossiped that it was because his daughters had left him, especially his favorite, Thérèse. Another suffering for the fervent religious was not to be able to receive the Eucharist daily. (Daily Eucharist became the norm after her death, which she correctly predicted.) But her greatest trial of all was one that took place in the deepest recesses of her soul.

Within two years of her entrance into Carmel, Thérèse began to experience a spiritual aridity that would accompany her for the remaining six years of her life. This kind of an experience is known as a dark night of the soul. It is a period of time in which God permits a person's faith, hope, and love to be put to the test as he prepares that individual for his future designs and great works—like gold tested in fire. During this ordeal, God allows only what a soul can handle and supports it with his grace throughout; otherwise the soul would perish in the suffering. In actuality, God is closer than ever to a soul, but the person has no concept of that; all he or she experiences is a sense of complete abandonment. Thérèse described the removal of God's sweet consolations as Jesus sound asleep in her little boat on a stormy sea—she knew he was there, but he was sleeping and not coming to her immediate rescue. This great interior trial brought her to the point of questioning whether heaven existed and God loved her. Fortunately, a good confessor helped her to navigate this spiritual storm and stay the course without joy as her compass. Her dark night would grow particularly intense in the final year of her life; but Thérèse barely talked about it, even in Confession, for fear of passing her indescribable torment on to others:

> Jesus made me feel that there were really souls who have no faith, and who, through the abuse of grace, lost this precious treasure, the source of the only real and pure joys. He permitted my soul to be invaded by the thickest darkness, and that the thought of heaven, up until then so sweet to me, be no longer anything but the cause of struggle and torment. (*Story of a Soul*, 211)

In the blackness, the evil one tempted her:

> You are dreaming about the light, about a fatherland embalmed in the sweetest perfumes; you are dreaming about the eternal possession of the Creator of all these marvels; you believe that one day you will walk out of this fog that surrounds you! Advance, advance; rejoice in death which will give you not what you hope for but a night still more profound, the night of nothingness. (*Story of a Soul*, 213)

Accompanying this spiritual trial were increased physical hardships. Thérèse suffered from tuberculosis of the lungs and intestines. While she was able, she performed her chores and practices, but much of her final year was spent "nailed in a bed of pain." Her last five months consisted of acute and ever-increasing agony, a slow suffocation and a final torture like that of Jesus on the cross. Through it all, she looked for ways to be a good and patient and consoling presence to her worried visitors. She trusted God wholly with her life, illness, and death, accepting every consolation and trial as a grace. She did not fear death but looked forward to heaven where she could love God all the more. Her final words were, "My God, I love you!" The spiritual darkness that had enshrouded Thérèse for so many years appeared to be lifted at the final moments of her life. As the community gathered around her bedside in prayer, she once more looked upon the statue of the Blessed Virgin that had miraculously healed her when she was ten. Her eyes were raised upward and fixed on a spot just above that statue. As the sisters watched, Thérèse's face came to life and radiated both joy and astonishment. She remained in that ecstasy long enough for the sisters to recite the Creed, and then she died with a beautiful smile on her face at the tender age of twenty-four.

The Unique Spirituality of St. Thérèse

Even in the years of spiritual emptiness, in which joy constantly eluded Thérèse, she made acts of faith and offered them for sinners and unbelievers. God was still leading his little daughter, but in a hidden way, helping her recognize traces of her self-love. The only antidote for this self-love, she discovered, was to become love for others. Thérèse also learned that the more a person advances spiritually, the more she sees the goal as still a long way off. She resigned to accept herself as imperfect and to find joy in this acceptance. Being love and being little became the basis of a spirituality that was uniquely hers.

It is due only to her famous autobiography, *Story of a Soul*, that the world has come to know the struggles, victories, and remarkable insights of this otherwise hidden saint-in-the making. She wrote the manuscript under obedience at the request of her sister, Pauline, who was the prioress of the community at the time. Originally, Thérèse wrote it as a family memoir or souvenir for her sisters, who loved to hear Thérèse recall stories of their childhood. She never intended for it to be shared with anyone else, let alone become a spiritual classic. The autobiography consists of three separate manuscripts. The first contains her childhood memories and entrance into Carmel, ending with Céline's entrance into the community six years later. The second and third manuscripts, written when she was already seriously ill and had the premonition that her writings would be a means of apostolate after her death, provide a glimpse into how marvelously expanded the heart and soul of this French nun had become.

For example, although Thérèse was deeply confirmed in her vocation as a Carmelite, her soul still yearned for more. She felt within herself the vocation of a warrior, ready to die on the battlefield in defense of the Church. She also felt the vocation of priest, desiring to call God down from heaven and give him to souls. She felt the vocation of missionary and apostle, anxious to preach God's name throughout the world, especially where it had not been preached before. She would have gladly shed her blood as a martyr if God had called her to that. Thérèse didn't see herself in any one of the members of the Body of Christ (as St. Paul described), but saw herself in all of them. Frustrated with her limitations and unmet ambitions, Thérèse finally came to the awareness that all of these vocational desires were grounded in the same thing—love:

> I understood that the Church has a heart, and that this heart was burning with love. I understood it was love alone that made the Church's members act, that if love ever became extinct, apostles would not preach the Gospel and martyrs would not shed their blood. I understood that love comprised all vocations, that love was everything, that it embraced all times and places . . . in a word, that it was eternal! Then, in the excess of my delirious joy, I cried out:

"O Jesus, my love . . . my vocation, at last I have found it . . .
my vocation is love!" (Story of a Soul, 194)

Thérèse would offer herself spiritually as a victim to
God's love through an oath-prayer she wrote and eventually
shared with some of the other sisters in the order. She called
it her "Act of Oblation to Merciful Love" (see appendix 2).
"To offer oneself as a victim of love," she explained in her
writings, "is to offer oneself to suffering, because love lives
only on sacrifice; so, if one is completely dedicated to loving,
one must expect to sacrifice unreservedly." Thérèse wanted
to die of love, and God ultimately took her up on this offer.

The Little Way

Contrary to common religious thinking in her time, Thérèse
discovered in scripture a compassionate God who welcomed
sinners and little ones. All that was necessary was to totally
abandon one's self to God's merciful love. She discovered a
way to attain sanctity by a path that all could recognize and
claim as their own. She called this way of trust and absolute
surrender her "little way." It was inspired by verses from
the Bible that emphasized the importance of littleness, such
as the need to become like little children to attain heaven
(Mt 18:3–4), and the way of spiritual childhood that leads to
eternal life (Mk 10:14–45).

Thérèse had no problem recognizing her littleness. She
compared the difference between herself and great saints
as a grain of sand to a mighty mountain. Still she aspired to
holiness and was determined to achieve it. "I want to seek
out a means of going to heaven by a little way, a way that is
very straight, very short, and totally new." The clever nun
was inspired by the advent of the elevator, a recent techno-
logical invention that helped people overcome stairs. Since
she considered herself too small to climb the rough stairway

of spiritual perfection, she sought an elevator to raise herself to Jesus. In the pages of scripture, she found her answer. Pondering the words, "Whoever is a little one, let him come to me" (Prv 9:4), Thérèse realized she didn't have to achieve great things to attain heaven. She simply had to remain little and Jesus' arms would be the elevator to lift her up.

This little way was not a timid, fearful way of approaching God, but one full of childlike boldness. It centered on seeking out everyday, ordinary events in life to find opportunities to do heroic acts of charity. It was a way that could lead one easily to progress and perfection. Thérèse recognized what others of her time had not: that the way to holiness was not something that could be attained by one's own efforts. It required these actions, done with love, but it also depended on God reaching down with his grace and transforming ordinary lives. His gifts of grace, love, and mercy were freely given and available to all. Holiness was available to all. Thérèse yearned with all her heart for souls to love God as she had come to love him and trust in his infinite mercy.

A Mission to Save Souls

Toward the end of her short life, Thérèse had a presentiment that her mission to save souls and share with them her ordinary way of trust and surrender would continue after her earthly life. She seemed to know this mission would involve more than just the influence of her book; it would consist of her heavenly intercession. This thought was inspired by one of her favorite saints, Stanislaus Kostka, who had a conversation with the Blessed Mother about wanting to do good on earth after his death, a request God granted him. Thérèse echoed St. Stanislaus's desire on her deathbed:

> I will return! I will come down! I feel that my mission is
> about to begin, my mission of making others love God as I

have loved him, my mission of teaching my little ways to
souls. If God answers my requests, my heaven will be spent
on earth until the end of the world. Yes, I want to spend
my heaven in doing good on earth. (*Story of a Soul*, 263)

Another saint who inspired her was Aloysius Gonzaga.
In a book about his life, we read how a certain sick man saw
a shower of roses fall on his bed. He saw this shower as a
sign that his prayer for a cure, through the intercession of St.
Aloysius, would be answered. Later, Thérèse confided to her
sisters, "I, too, will let fall a shower of roses after my death."
A year after Thérèse's death, her manuscript was published
and sent to other Carmels in lieu of an obituary. The Carmels
shared the book with others and soon requests for books,
relics, pictures, and novena leaflets came flooding into the
convent. The book quickly became a bestseller in several languages. Pilgrims began to pray at the gravesite of Thérèse
and reported cures, conversions, and favors—including flowers and the scent of flowers—attributed to her intercession.
Thousands of letters arrived at the Lisieux Carmel attesting to
similar miracles. Numerous people reported that Thérèse was
like a guardian angel to them, providing them with continual
assistance. The example of her life and love for God seemed
to reawaken and increase their fervor for spiritual perfection.
Her writings inspired many holy vocations, and missionary
work in Asia and other foreign locations flourished.

The impact of Thérèse's life of heroic virtue led to her
canonization in 1925. Since then, she has become universally
loved and arguably the greatest saint of modern times. Her
titles include Patroness of Missionaries, Secondary Patroness
of France (equal to St. Joan of Arc), and Doctor of the Church
(conferred by Blessed John Paul II in 1997). Her relics, which
continue to tour the world, draw in great numbers of people
of all ages, faiths, and walks of life. Certainly it can be said
that she has achieved her mission to make God better known

and loved. People continue to be attracted to Thérèse's way of love and trust in God and find in her example the encouragement they need to travel this way without fear. For them, she is an accessible saint who seems to obtain the hidden graces they need to help them toward perfection. Thérèse shows people how to cover their crucifixes with flowers and smile in the face of suffering. Based on the ageless teaching of the gospels, her message remains as vital today. Yes, she was given exceptional grace from God, but equally important, she responded to it with an exceptional degree of correspondence that will be fully appreciated only in the world to come.

The Virtue of Love

As Thérèse admits in her autobiography, she was raised in love. It was a language spoken well by her family and the means by which she learned to feel and respond to God's presence in her life, even as a small child. This love for God grew as she grew. Her desire was to love Jesus with a passion, to give him a thousand proofs of her love. Love became her vocation. Thérèse came to understand that at the end of the day, it is only love that makes us acceptable to God. She was prepared to love him into folly, she would say. Her dream was to die of love, but in order to die of love, she knew she must first live by love.

For Thérèse, love wasn't reduced to a feeling; it was a conscious decision to practice virtue and please God in the least of her actions while trying not to draw attention to herself. As Thérèse matured in her faith, she realized it wasn't enough to love God with a love that was hidden in the bottom of her heart. Her love had to be extended to others. In her religious community, she accepted the fact that she hadn't loved her sisters in the Carmel with the perfect love that God loved them. She was incapable of loving them that much until she realized that Jesus could love them in her.

Yes, I feel it, when I am charitable, it is Jesus alone who is acting in me, and the more united I am to him, the more also do I love my Sisters. When I wish to increase this love in me, and when especially the devil tries to place before the eyes of my soul the faults of such and such a Sister who is less attractive to me, I hasten to search out her virtues, her good intentions. (*Story of a Soul,* 221)

Thérèse learned that without love, all works are nothing and love is nourished only by sacrifices. She accepted all her sufferings in a spirit of love for the sake of the souls she wanted to win over to the love of God. She had an interesting ritual at the start of her day to demonstrate her decision to nurture love in herself and others. Each morning she kissed her crucifix and placed it gently on her pillow while she dressed. She would tell Jesus, "Look, you worked and wept enough for thirty-three years here on earth; today you can take a rest, it's my turn to fight and suffer."

At a time when religion seemed to focus on God's justice and his swift punishment for sin, Thérèse looked to the gospels and saw a compassionate God who loved sinners, tax collectors, prostitutes, lepers, and little ones like herself. She didn't live in fear of God's punishment in this life or the next, as many of her contemporaries did. She understood that God's ever-burning fire of love was more sanctifying for the soul than any fire in purgatory, and she chose to remain close to that burning love at all times. That's why she offered herself as a victim of holocaust to God's merciful love. If it were God's will, Thérèse would have even gone to hell among those eternal flames, just so he could have a soul who would love him from that dismal place.

Thérèse saw how transforming God's love could be on a soul and how important it was to maintain this connection with him at all times. Again, she used nature to illustrate this point:

I saw through the window the setting sun casting its last fierce rays over nature, and the tops of the trees seemed gilded. Then I thought: what a difference it makes whether you remain in the shade or expose yourself to the sun of love, in the latter case one becomes golden all over. That is why I look all gilded, whereas in reality I am not, and I would immediately cease to appear so if I estranged myself from love. (Christopher O'Mahony, *St. Thérèse of Lisieux,* 101)

Not only did Thérèse uncover the loving and compassionate Jesus of the gospels, she made the startling discovery of how much Jesus himself desired to be loved. This was certainly radical thinking for her time:

Jesus is parched, for he meets only the ungrateful and indifferent among his disciples in the world and among his own disciples. Alas, he finds few hearts who surrender to him without reservations, who understand the real tenderness of his infinite heart. (*Story of a Soul,* 94)

Thérèse wanted nothing more than to console her Jesus and for others to share this desire. To please Jesus and enrapture his heart was easy, she claimed in her writings. One had only to love him without looking at oneself and without spending too much time examining one's faults.

Among the many heroic virtues that led to the proclamation of her sainthood, it is love that was best mastered by St. Thérèse of Lisieux. Love was all she asked for; it was the only skill she needed. Through this virtue, she unlocked the mystery of knowing, consoling, and serving God in the ordinary details of life. Her little way of love has changed millions of lives and is the reason she herself is one of the best-loved saints of all time.

LESSONS IN LOVE
FROM THÉRÈSE

The first time I read Thérèse's autobiography, *Story of a Soul*, I was a relatively new Catholic. I read it out of curiosity, as part of my fact-finding mission to discover more about the woman on the religious medal in my jewelry box. What I found, however, was far more than facts. From the first pages of her autobiography, despite our ethnic, cultural, and historical differences, St. Thérèse of Lisieux captured my heart and my imagination. The more I read about her childhood experiences, trials and triumphs, and intense passion for God, the more I felt as if I had always known her. Her spiritual insights seemed to awaken something deep inside me. It was as if she were reminding me of truths that I had always known deep down, but had not really considered. In many ways, Thérèse validated my own personal relationship with God, which had started in childhood. She showed me how to take that relationship so much further.

At the time I was reading Thérèse's autobiography, saints were becoming helpful guideposts in my spiritual journey, but I was still pretty intimidated by their state of holiness compared to my many shortcomings. Thérèse broke through that for me. It's not that she didn't achieve near perfection in my eyes—she did! But what drew me to St. Thérèse was her vulnerability in revealing who she was at the core, flaws and all, and how she had come to accept herself without false pretensions. She struggled with the challenges of life—abandonment, self-doubt, illness, and difficult relationships—just like the rest of us, but she used those challenges as opportunities for growth. Hers was an open invitation to put ourselves—just as we are—completely in God's hands. While I wasn't quite ready to take the total leap of faith she had taken, her story gave me the courage and desire to give God just a little bit more of me.

Thérèse's claim at the end of her life that she would do good on earth after her death a captivating concept that illuminated for me the reality of saintly intercession. This wasn't just the claim of a dying woman. Thérèse demonstrated faithfulness to her promise over and over, in countless ways and in as many lives. I believe she did it for me, personally, when I found her medal on the sidewalk. Through that ordinary and simple means, she quietly entered my life to guide me in my journey and become my spiritual journey partner. Thérèse took me by the hand spiritually and whispered secrets to me about being a better follower of Jesus. She helped me believe that I could find a way to love God more deeply in my own ordinary living. She pushed me to be a more fervent Catholic. Then she did something even more extraordinary. She invited me—a stumbling convert—to consider evangelizing others.

The Pilgrimage

If I were to describe my faith walk in my first years of being Catholic in the 1980s, it would be swift and with definite direction. In those years I was happily immersed in reading and studying the Catholic faith and learning of the great ones who had come before me. I felt I was making comfortable and steady progress spiritually, but what I didn't realize at the time was that my faith was myopic and self-centered. Perhaps influenced by the "me generation" of that decade, I was in it for myself, to learn what I could and to try to be more pleasing to God. Despite my good intentions and outwardly "holy" behavior, I often let my romance with my new Catholic faith come before my romance with my husband Mark. This caused strife and division between us. I resented my husband's seeming lack of interest in our faith—the faith, after all, that was his first and that he had invited me into—and at times I felt he hindered me. I wanted to run, as Thérèse had seemed to run, but the more I ran, the more Mark seemed to drag his feet. One day, he shared with me that he felt like he was choking on my dust. Those words were hard for me to hear, but they made me realize that I had violated the example of love that Thérèse had shown me. I had failed to include my spouse on the journey and make my faith pursuit attractive to him. As I pondered how to rectify this, God provided an answer in the form of my first experience of pilgrimage.

Looking back, I'm not sure how exactly I was able to convince my husband to travel with me to a communist country in Eastern Europe where a reported apparition was taking place in a small village called Medjugorje. We had never traveled outside of the country, let alone to such a remote and potentially volatile destination, where political tensions were on the rise. The idea was crazy, daring, and at the same time, irresistible. I remember how Mark did not initially share my enthusiasm. It wasn't because he doubted this event could be authentic; in fact, he was pretty open to the idea of a modern-day Marian apparition. It wasn't even the idea of going into a troubled communist country that bothered him. His hesitancy stemmed from the fear that a pilgrimage like this could demand change and conversion, and he was nervous about what God might be asking of us. In short, he liked his life the way it was. In the end, though, he and his entire family agreed to make the journey. That pilgrimage illustrated for me the true universality of the Church, which I had not understood before. It was a place of near-perfect faith and unity, like heaven on earth; I was disappointed at the thought of returning to the real world when our pilgrimage was over.

Living the Messages

What I learned after my return from Medjugorje was that I didn't have to allow my pilgrimage to disappear into the shadows of my memories. I found out that pilgrimage was an opportunity for us to leave a part of ourselves behind— our former selves—and come back to our relationships and situations as new and revitalized people, as better followers of Christ. In the aftermath of our trip, Mark and I decided we would do our best to apply the key messages of the reported apparitions to our lives, keeping our pilgrimage alive in our hearts. There were five basic calls to action: daily prayer (particularly the Rosary), daily time with sacred scripture, frequent reception of the Eucharist (daily if possible), weekly fasting (particularly on bread and water), and monthly Confession. Implementing these actions had immediate effects on our relationship with God and his Church. Living these messages over time has helped my husband and me bond spiritually in a way we had not been able to do on our own. We both became more on fire about our Catholic faith. Together, we started a faith-sharing group in our home, and we also developed an acute interest in apologetics to be able to explain and defend the faith. We took pleasure in practicing our faith as a couple and sharing our spiritual enthusiasm with our growing family.

Our pilgrimage had one other important and lasting effect on me, and I think this is where I felt the influence of Thérèse resurface in my life. Just days after our return, I was typing up my journal notes from the trip while the events were still fresh in my mind. A friend asked if she could read them. At first, I was reluctant because they were personal, like a diary. But I decided to take a risk and share them with her because I knew she was struggling in her own faith. Soon after, I had other requests for a copy of my journal. At the same time, I was asked to give a witness talk at my parish about why I am Catholic, and I included a small part of the pilgrimage in my testimony.

As I took these initial shaky steps to move out of my comfort zone and share my faith with others, I began to see a positive response; people were hungry for this. God was leading me in a new direction. He was showing me that my zeal for learning and living my faith was no longer meant to be a personal journey of self-discovery for only my family and myself. It was something much bigger—it was something to be shared. For the first time, I felt the bud of desire to help others grow in their faith and understanding of God. I wanted others to experience God's love for them in the personal way I felt his love for me. These were the exact aspirations of St. Thérèse, and this realization confirmed in my mind that she had been brought into my life for a reason.

Discovering My Mission

As I was feeling the sparks of something new and exciting happening in my faith life, I wanted, at the same time, to be sure I wasn't running off willy-nilly with my own ideas. If this were truly God's call for me, he needed to be in charge and show me exactly how I was to carry out this mission of evangelization. I began to pray for that intention. It was a short prayer, nothing deeply insightful or dramatic, and something I often uttered while I was driving to work: "Lord, help me to be an instrument of your will. Help me to glorify you by bringing souls to you like Thérèse did. Help me to set people on fire with love for you. And Lord—you can do this in any way you want." This last part of the prayer was the greatest act of faith for me. Interiorly, I wanted God to use me as a writer since he had already given me a talent in that area, but I knew that for this to be truly his mission and not mine, I had to let him drive. I had to let go of the wheel and be content to sit in the passenger seat until he acted. Faithfully, I kept praying this little prayer intention every day, and God did answer it—ten years later. (That's when I learned the hard lesson that God doesn't always answer prayers on our schedule!)

A lot happened in those ten years. For starters, we had three boys. I had also transitioned from full-time work to part-time work to freelance writing to being a full-time stay-at-home mom. My fortieth birthday was approaching, and I was ready to enter a new chapter in my life. I was anxious to get away from freelance advertising writing and try my hand at authoring books. My dream was to write a secular children's book. I went so far as to attend some conferences on how to write for children. In between nursing my youngest, changing diapers, and handling all the other tasks of managing a busy household and family, I wrote clever and charming manuscripts, and I fantasized about being a successful author. Each time I sent a story out, though the answer was always the same: no. No thank you. Cute, but no. Can't use it. Try again. It was getting pretty discouraging. Finally,

I got the inspiration to totally switch gears and write a magazine article for adults. It was the story of a little miracle that had happened to my son and me, involving the intercession of my spiritual journey partner, St. Thérèse.

By Any Other Name

The story took place when our oldest son, Michael, was in second grade. I was rereading the autobiography of St. Thérèse one afternoon when I heard the sound of his slow, shuffling footsteps and a book bag being dragged down the hallway; he was home and he wasn't happy. When I asked what was wrong, he foraged grumpily through his overstuffed book bag and produced a wrinkled homework assignment from the center pocket. He was to talk to his parents about their favorite saint and report on it the following week.

Hiding my smile, I peered at my son's downcast face. "Well, now, that doesn't sound too bad." Michael grunted in response. I leaned over and picked up the book I had just been revisiting, *Story of a Soul*, and gazed at the sweet, smiling face of Thérèse on the cover. I couldn't help but smile back at the irony that she had introduced herself to me when I was in second grade, and now she was about to enter the consciousness of my second-grade son.

I told Michael that St. Thérèse of Lisieux was my favorite saint and one I believed had been keeping an eye on me since I was his age. When I asked if he would like to know a little about her, he shrugged his shoulders and looked about as enthusiastic as if I had asked him to choose between Brussels sprouts or lima beans for dinner. Undaunted, I told my son about St. Thérèse's spunky personality as a child, how her older sisters raised her after her mother had died, and how she became a Carmelite nun at the young age of fifteen. I talked a little about her surpassing virtue and her little way of loving God as a merciful father, which all of us could follow. Michael began to fidget.

"You know," I said, adding a bit of drama to my voice, "St. Thérèse said something very interesting before she died." Michael looked up at me for the first time with inquisitive eyes. "She said that after her death she would let fall a shower of roses."

Michael's fidgeting stopped, and I continued by telling him how Thérèse got the nickname of the "Little Flower" because she loved flowers and used to look at the world as if it were a flower garden and she were the smallest flower of all. She made a promise to her community that after she had died and gone to heaven, she would continue to do good work here on earth. I spoke about how a tradition began after her death. People started to pray and ask the Little Flower for help with their special needs. They asked Thérèse to go before God on their behalf and present him with their requests. Many times people would receive a flower shortly after they had made their prayer to St. Thérèse. They took it as a sign that their prayers had been heard. I shared with Michael the fact that it had even happened to me.

"It did?" Now I had Michael's full attention. He took the book from my hands to look at the woman who could do such marvelous things. I proceeded to describe an experience that had happened to me the year before. I had been on retreat, and during my days in silence, I was plagued with a burning question about my deceased mother, wondering if she had made it to heaven after all these years. On the last day of the retreat, I turned my attention to Thérèse. I asked her this question in prayer and gathered up the nerve to ask for the affirmation of a red rose. I was hesitant to make this request because I was afraid of being superstitious or weak in faith. It was still one of those Catholic traditions that felt strange and uncomfortable to me as a former Protestant. As soon as my prayer was uttered, however, a little red bird landed in the tree outside of my window in the retreat house and began to sing loudly. "Is this my sign?" I wondered, even though I had asked for a red rose, not a red bird. A moment later, a young seminarian, dressed in a bright red sweater strolled down the walk. "Or that?" I puzzled. Even the clouds around the sun seemed to have a reddish glow about them that afternoon. Convinced I was seeing things and feeling pretty silly, I laughed and got up to go to the closing Mass.

The Mass was the perfect ending to my retreat, and afterward I joined the other retreatants in the dining hall for our final meal together. On each plate was a folded prayer card with the picture of St. Thérèse of Lisieux on the cover. With trembling hands, I opened the card, and a small silk red rose slipped out into my lap. Tears sprang to my eyes as I believed my prayer had been answered. Ever since that moment, I've not had any more doubts about the where-abouts of my mother—or Thérèse, for that matter.

"Can I do that?" Michael asked, incredulously, after hearing my story. "Can I ask St. Thérèse for something and have her answer me with a flower?"

I was pleased by my son's interest and excitement. I assured him he could, trying to make my voice sound a little more confident than I was actually feeling inside. After all, you can't force miracles, and I didn't want my son to be dis-appointed just in case this little experiment didn't work out. I asked him if there was a question he wanted to ask Thérèse.

"Yes," he said. "I want to know if Mrs. Reed is in heaven."

Michael's swift and serious response caught me off guard. I had expected him to ask something more childlike, such as if he were going to get a bike for his birthday. I had no idea that my young son still had such concern for the beloved neighbor and surrogate grandmother who had passed away months earlier.

With emotion, I told Michael to ask. Suddenly, his cheeks flushed and he became very shy. He wanted me to do the asking for him. I laughed and pulled him close. This was turning into such a beautiful mother/son moment. "All right," I said, becoming more serious. "St. Thérèse, Michael would like to ask your intercession on something. He wants to know if our neighbor, Mrs. Reed, is in heaven yet. Uhh . . . Amen."

"You forgot the part about the flower," Michael insisted.

"Oh, yes. My son would also like to ask you to send him a flower in response to his prayer."

"So, where is it?" demanded Michael, half-seriously.

"You have to give it time," I replied, "and let St. Thérèse do her work."

Two mornings later, in the hustle and bustle of busy family life, I had forgotten all about our conversation with St. Thérèse and the flower. I was in the upstairs bathroom getting ready for the day, when I was brought to rapt attention by the insistent yelling of my son. "Mom? Mom!" Michael's screams were coming from the kitchen. Panicked, I practically flew downstairs, recognizing the tone in my son's voice that said, "This is really important!"

When I arrived in the kitchen out of breath, I found Michael jumping up and down yelling about how his prayer had been answered, how he got his flower, and how Mrs. Reed was in heaven. Dumbfounded by the commotion and relieved at the same time that he wasn't hurt, I followed the direction of his insistent pointed finger. There on the kitchen table, in a vase, stood a single yellow rose.

For a moment, my mouth hung open as I tried to process all of this; then the pieces fell into place. Our weekly faith-sharing group had gathered in our home the night before. As usual, Mr. Reed had brought a flower with him to represent the presence of his deceased wife. He often brought a yellow rose—her favorite—and this particular one was cut from a rose bush we had planted in his wife's honor. After our guests had left and my husband and I were cleaning up, I realized Mr. Reed had accidentally left his flower behind. I was going to return it to him, but the hour was late and I decided I could return it in the morning. I had placed the flower on the kitchen table and went to bed, never giving it another thought.

For Michael, the mechanics of how this flower arrived at our home was not at all important. The only thing that mattered to him was this simple yellow rose, specially delivered to him by a heavenly messenger who cared.

"Yes," I answered, choking back my tears as I made the mental connections. "St. Thérèse certainly has answered your prayer. Not only did she send you a flower, she sent you one from Mrs. Reed's rose bush! What better sign could you get that Mrs. Reed is in heaven?"

As we hugged, I marveled at how this all had worked out. The real miracle for me was seeing Michael accept it all so easily. I knew right then and there that he would never look at saints in the same way again. His life would be greatly enriched by believing confidently in their intercession, and I could only imagine what he would share in his classroom discussion on the saints.

A Writing Ministry

After I penned a version of this story, I sent it out to *Catholic Parent* magazine on a whim. With all the rejections I had received from various book publishers for my children's stories, I really wasn't expecting much. In fact, I had pretty much dismissed it. Then one afternoon, I was lying on the couch in our living room with a crushing headache. It was the kind of pounding pain that knocked me off my feet. As I lay there feeling sorry for myself, I wondered what was wrong with me. My mind kicked around crazy thoughts: it was either a brain tumor or I was pregnant again—at the age of forty. I'm not proud to say that the brain-tumor idea was sounding more appealing at the time. I know moms are supposed to be absolutely thrilled at each discovery of pregnancy, but I was not at all in that place. I was exhausted with three young boys and I had my hopes on taking up writing again. I wanted and needed to have some time for me. It was a selfish thought, not virtuous at all, but that's where I was emotionally. The more I thought about the reality of being pregnant at that age and what others might say or think, the angrier I grew with God that he could let this happen to me.

It was at that moment that my husband burst through the door with the mail in his hands and a beaming smile on his face. "Honey!" he announced excitedly, "you're published!" I just lay there with a dumb look on my face. I had no idea what he was ranting about. "Look," he said triumphantly waving a letter in my face. "*Catholic Parent* magazine loved your article and they're going to publish it. You're an author!"

I took the letter from him, trying not to sit up too quickly and set off another round of tom-toms in my head. I squinted my eyes at the word, "yes." I'd never seen that word before from a publisher. Headache and all, I suddenly realized that the door I had been desperately trying to open in the publishing world was finally opening—it was just a different door. I was to be an author—but not a secular one. I was to be a Catholic author. God was taking me up on my ten-year prayer and giving me the green light now, at forty years of age with a fourth child on the way (as my doctor would later confirm). At this crazy, unexpected, and surprising time of my life, my writing ministry was launched; and Thérèse was at the heart of it all.

The Book

After the article was published in January 2000, I began to get the most interesting calls and e-mails. People contacted me to tell me how much they had enjoyed my story and proceeded to tell me about a special intercession they had experienced with the help of the Little Flower. It didn't take me long to figure out that this flowery phenomenon was pretty popular, and I began to feel prompted to turn these stories into a book. After getting the interest of a publisher in New York, I sent out a call for stories via the Internet. Within twenty-four hours, my first response came in—from Brazil. I had not even considered I would get stories from outside of the United States, but it confirmed all the more for me the contemporary appeal and universality of St. Thérèse of Lisieux. There were stories of finding long-lost relatives, landing new jobs, dealing with the loss of a baby, attempting to get pregnant, forgiving family members, finding love, healing miraculously, converting, and finding spiritual guidance. Each time, Thérèse showed herself as a responsive, compassionate, and loving friend from heaven. It really opened my eyes to how influential and personal she was in so many people's journeys.

In the midst of collecting and editing the stories for this project, I landed a contract with another publisher for a series of Catholic children's books. My mission of book writing was now in full swing. My prayers to evangelize like Thérèse had been answered in a viable way for my state in life as a stay-at-home mother.

Her Impact Today

Story of a Soul is a book that can be visited and revisited. Each time I read it, I gain a little more insight. Each time it inspires me to take a few more steps in the direction of holiness and virtue. Each time, the saint's invitation is gentle, but I feel as though the more I read her wisdom, the more I am accountable for applying it. As Luke 12:48 tells us, to those whom much has been given, much will be required. On a recent reading of Thérèse's autobiography for the preparation of this book, I felt her teaching me to go deeper, stretch myself more. It's as if I've become one of the novices she used to mentor. She is firm with me without ever losing her charity. She holds my feet to the fire, but with gentleness and love. She still accepts me for who I am, with my impatience, desire for control, and self-absorptive tendencies, but continues to invite me to love my husband, my sons, and those I encounter with a deeper and more self-giving love. As my first spiritual journey partner, Thérèse will always hold a special place in the recesses of my heart, but God soon showed me that she would not be the only saint to take residence there.

OCEANS
OF MERCY

I first heard the name Blessed Faustina Kowalska in 1995 from my mother-in-law, who had learned about this extraordinary mystic nun through a Polish friend in New Jersey. I remember my mother-in-law being very animated in her descriptions of how this humble religious sister of the 1930s received messages from Jesus Christ about his divine mercy. She was so inspired by these messages that she gave out little images and articles about them to many of her friends and relatives who had grown lukewarm in their faith. My mother-in-law experienced a great hope embodied in the words of Jesus to Faustina, and she yearned to reach out to others she loved to remind them that God's mercy is available to all.

Impressed at her grassroots evangelization efforts, I borrowed my mother-in-law's copy of Faustina's diary, *Divine*

Mercy in My Soul, and upon reading it, I instantly understood the reason for my mother-in-law's enthusiasm about this devotion. In page after page, I felt like a privileged audience, listening to the wisdom and counsel of Jesus Christ himself as he prepared and instructed this otherwise ordinary nun for one of the greatest missions in history: to spread the message of divine mercy to the world.

As I think about it now, I had only been in the Church two years when I read Faustina's writings for the first time. Rather than being overwhelmed by this woman's zeal for spiritual perfection and discouraged at the mountain of difference between her willingness to suffer and mine, I was enraptured by this message of mercy. Here was God, in modern times—in my time—pleading for the world to approach him, the unfathomable font of mercy, to be healed and renewed. No matter what the sin, or more importantly, how great the sin, he was offering us the ultimate do-over. It was the promise of a second chance for a world that had largely gone astray.

I, like my mother-in-law, felt eager to share the message of hope I had discovered in Faustina's writings, so I set about putting together a presentation for my faith-sharing group that my husband and I belonged to in those days. I took some careful notes from the diary, found a short video on Jesus, the Divine Mercy at a local Catholic bookstore, and purchased some holy cards with the image of the Divine Mercy to distribute to the other young couples in our group. At the time, my passion to share what I had learned from *Divine Mercy in My Soul* was fueled by a desire to help bring others closer to God, an aspiration implanted by my first spiritual journey partner, Thérèse. I had no idea that all along God (and Faustina) were preparing me to experience the Divine Mercy in a real and powerful way in my own life. They knew that for me to be an effective agent in bringing this message to a wider audience (which would be a part of my future mission), it would be best for me to experience that grace firsthand.

Miracle of Mercy

As I was finalizing the details of my upcoming presentation to our faith-sharing group, I was also engaged in many elements of the Divine Mercy devotion. For example, I had displayed a small image of the Divine Mercy on my desk, I was praying the special prayer Jesus taught Faustina for nine consecutive days, and I was anticipating going to Confession the Sunday after Easter for the full remission of sins and the effects of those sins, as Jesus had promised to Faustina. Even though the Feast of Divine Mercy had not yet been established in the universal Church (this would not happen until the year 2001), I felt it was too important a grace to miss, so I made sure I marked the first Sunday after Easter on my calendar to celebrate God's gift of mercy.

Just as everything was going so wonderfully, disaster struck as I committed a most regrettable action. Our first son was four years old at the time, and our second was a newborn baby. He was the baby that never slept, at least not when the rest of the world was sleeping. Night after night he cried to be held and fed, and no matter what I did, he never seemed to close his eyes and settle down. He was awake, and, therefore, I was too. Too many of these sleep-deprived nights had taken a toll on me. I was short-tempered and feeling sorry for myself. One morning, our four-year-old, who I'm sure was feeling a bit put out by his baby brother's intrusion into the family but was too polite to say so, acted out in his own way by refusing to get ready for preschool. This in itself was certainly not a terrible crime, but for his bleary-eyed mother, it was the last straw. I totally lost it and raged against my four-year-old in a way that filled me with profound shame and regret. Devastated and shocked at how such an unbridled outburst could occur, especially during the onset of Holy Week, I felt demoted and defiled and worthy of the ranks of Peter the denier and Judas the betrayer. I felt unforgivable and like the worst mother in the world. Immediately, I knew I had to rectify things. First, I apologized to my son, who had been very shaken by the event. Next, I called my husband who was away on a business trip. It was the most difficult call I ever had to make. Finally, what I needed to do most of all was to make this better with God, and there was only one way to do it—through the means of Confession.

Confession Struggles

I was not big fan of Confession as a newly-minted Catholic. In fact, it was the single greatest obstacle I had in entering the Church in the first place. For some converts, the greatest obstacle is Jesus in the Eucharist. For others, it is the Blessed Virgin Mary. For me, it was the idea of going into one of those dark little closets with a complete stranger and telling him the worst and most embarrassing things about myself. I dreaded the whole process. In the Lutheran faith of my childhood, Confession was a public event. The congregation would stand and together recite from a book words that essentially said we were sorry. The pastor, acting on God's behalf, would read back words from the same book, essentially saying we were forgiven. It was easy and painless, but it never bore for me the kind of fruits that I would eventually discover through a Catholic Confession.

At the time of this incident with my son, Confession was still a major stumbling block. I would go once or twice a year in order to fulfill my obligation, but I dreaded every moment of it. Afterward, I never felt better. My problem was that I could not see beyond the man in the white collar sitting across from me to recognize that I was encountering Jesus Christ in this sacrament. Instead, I focused on the human being sitting and waiting for me in that stark wooden box. I imagined that priests probably carried a little black book in which they logged each person's sins and that perhaps they talked about these sins on the golf course or over coffee with their priest buddies. Convinced that, at the very least, my pastor would certainly not like me once he knew my sins, I would travel across town to visit another parish and make my confession there.

This time, however, I decided to go to my own parish and see my own pastor. I felt I needed the extra penance. With a sick feeling in my stomach, I drove my infant and myself to the church. There were two lines for Confession, a long line for a likable retired priest who would help out at the Masses, and a short line for the pastor who was known, at times, to be rather acrimonious. I took the short line and took a deep breath. My pulse quickened and I began to sweat as the line moved steadily forward. An elderly Italian woman came up to me with a smile and offered to hold my baby while I went into the confessional. I didn't even know the woman, but robotically handed him over, still feeling like the unfit mother. The next thing I knew, I was in the confessional.

As my pastor patiently listened, I let it all come out between big and ugly sobs. I relayed all the gory details and how absolutely ashamed I felt. He gave me a few words of advice and then moved on to absolution, as if I had told him I had inadvertently not paid for an item in the bottom of my grocery cart. I sat there on that little wooden chair, waiting for a punishment, a lecture, a dunce cap or something, but it did not come. The Confession was over and it was time to leave. Dazed and still wracked with guilt and pain, I felt as though the weight of the world was on my shoulders. I still felt unforgiven, undeserving, and generally despicable; and it took every bit of energy for me to rise from the chair. That's when a most amazing miracle happened.

As I was exiting the confessional to return to the sanctuary, I felt as though someone had placed a bucket of warm water on the threshold above the doorway. Suddenly, I felt the physical sensation of water splashing over me and washing me clean. In a moment—a nanosecond—I felt such an incredible sense of joy, peace, and lightness that I even looked down at my feet to see if I were floating. It was such a complete and instantaneous transformation from what I had been feeling a moment prior, and it was so completely unanticipated that I knew God had to be behind it. It was as though he was acknowledging how contrite I had been over what I had done and he was happy to welcome me back. This, he wanted me to know, was what his genuine healing and forgiveness felt like. I recalled the words he imparted to Faustina: "I pour out a whole ocean of graces upon those souls who approach the fount of my mercy . . . all the divine floodgates through which graces flow are opened."

That day, for reasons I cannot explain and certainly do not deserve, I was privileged to experience a tangible example of the power of God's love and mercy. This experience made Faustina's words come alive in a deeper and more meaningful way, and it forever changed my attitude about Confession. It gave me great hope that I could be forgiven and start over, like a slate washed clean. God's ocean of mercy was big enough to do that, and it was there just for the asking. As difficult as it was for me to walk through this particular trial, I will be forever grateful for the grace and lessons it taught me and for how this incident would be used to help others place their hope and trust in God's unfathomable mercy. Before I relate that story, I would like to tell the story of my second spiritual journey partner, St. Faustina.

FAUSTINA:
A VISION OF HOPE

Helena Kowalska was born to a poor and pious peasant family in Glogowiec, a small village in the heart of Poland. She was the third of ten children, raised by a father who was a farmer and carpenter and a mother who was hard working and loving. Helena's parents had a simple but deep and living Catholic faith that they passed on to their children, teaching them how to put divine matters first. Their religious instruction included understanding strict fasting, learning short prayers, and listening to stories from the Bible or about saints. Even from her youngest years, Helena was attracted to longer periods of prayer and contemplation than were her siblings.

Her first experience of God calling her to a more perfect life, she would recall later in her diary, happened when she was a small child.

Once, when I was seven years old, at a Vesper Service, conducted before the Lord Jesus in the monstrance, the love of God was imparted to me for the first time and filled my little heart; and the Lord gave me understanding of divine things. (Maria Faustina Kowalska, *Divine Mercy in My Soul*, 499)

This was a tremendous grace, but since Helena was so small—still two years away from receiving First Holy Communion—and because she didn't have anyone to explain these things to her, she didn't always respond to that grace. The event, however, instilled in her heart a desire to become a religious, but she kept this dream hidden from the world.

To her family, Helena was known for her piety, industriousness, obedience, and a great sensitivity to human misery. She made contrite confessions every week and enjoyed reading stories about the saints to neighborhood children, even acting them out with great drama. She loved going to church on Sundays, but since World War I had left the family destitute, her parents couldn't afford proper church clothing for all the children. Helena and her sisters shared one good dress and had to take turns going to church. On her day home, Helena would read her prayer book and pray.

At twelve years of age, Helena was sent to school, though her schooling was shortlived. Due to the Russian occupation of Poland, many schools were closed and the older students were ordered to leave. After three school terms, Helena was sent home. This would be the extent of her formal education.

By the age of fourteen, Helena started seeing strange bright lights during prayer. She shared this information with her parents, who were convinced her imagination was the cause. Hesitantly, she also confided her desire to enter a convent, but her parents flatly refused. She was too young and was needed at home to help with the younger children. A year later, Helena was sent to work as a domestic to help support her family. Her prayer life deepened and she continued seeing strange lights. Eventually, she returned to ask her parents again about religious life, and for the second time, they refused. They were not anxious to lose their favorite daughter, and besides, they had no money to provide a dowry.

Thinking religious life was closed to her, Helena turned to worldly things, despite her inner promptings to the contrary. She engaged in fashion and dances, but none of this made her happy. At the age of eighteen, she found another domestic job in the nearby city of Lodz. During this time, she attended a dance with her sister and experienced her first supernatural vision, a striking manifestation of the suffering Christ. With pitiful eyes he asked her, "How long shall I put up with you, and how long will you keep putting me off?" Helena was shaken by this vision. Feigning a headache, she immediately excused herself from the party and went to the Cathedral of St. Stanislaus Kostka to pray. Interiorly, she heard the words, "Go at once to Warsaw; you will enter a convent there." Helena could no longer run away from her Lord. She left for Warsaw with only the clothes on her back. She told her sister and an uncle, and asked them to bid farewell to her parents. She knew her parents would be heartbroken and think she had run away, but her need to be obedient to God, whom she had come to love, took precedence.

In Warsaw, Helena was guided to safe lodging. She knocked on the door of several convents in the city and was repeatedly turned away until she approached the Congregation of the Sisters of Our Lady of Mercy. The superior there accepted the young girl under the condition that she remain in the world for one year working as a domestic to earn her dowry. That year would be a time of great struggle for Helena as she longed for the convent, but it was also a time when God filled her soul with a deeper knowledge of him as supreme goodness and beauty. To prepare for religious life, she fasted strictly and did acts of mortification.

Entrance into Religious Life

Helena was formally accepted into the Congregation of the Sisters of Our Lady of Mercy on August 1, 1925. On that day, she felt as though she had walked into paradise. Three weeks later, however, her bliss was obliterated with an intense temptation to leave the order for another community that spent more time in prayer. Helena did not know what to do. Finally, Jesus manifested his wounded and tortured face to her on the curtain that separated her dormitory bed from the others. "It is you who will cause me this pain if you leave this convent. It is to this place that I called you and nowhere else, and it is here I have prepared many graces for you." Hearing those words, Helena resolved to stay.

Because of the zealous fasting and mortification she had put herself through before entering religious life, Helena had to be nursed back to health during her first year at the convent. Despite that fact, she moved rapidly through her postulancy, finishing it in Cracow to begin her novitiate. On April 30, 1926, Helena received the habit and veil and the religious name Sister Maria Faustina, a name that means "fortunate, happy, or blessed one." At the same time, Jesus showed Faustina in a vision how much she was to suffer, but he also gave her great consolations that provided her the strength to accept the suffering.

The Dark Night

Sister Maria Faustina's novitiate was a two-year process. The first year was designed to deepen a sister's spiritual life through meditation and other spiritual practices. This was the time to study the rules of the order and practice virtues, especially the virtue of humility. In the second year, studies were added to the practice of spiritual exercises. Toward the end of her first year of novitiate, Faustina experienced a dark night of the soul. She was one of the few saints to put pen to paper to describe this excruciating time of suffering. Her dark night began when God removed his consolations. She no longer heard his voice, saw his face, or felt his presence. It became difficult for her to meditate. Fear swept over her, and she saw only misery and imperfections in herself, which left her begging God for mercy. The novice director tried to encourage Faustina, thinking she was being overly scrupulous, but the young sister's suffering only grew. The simple truths of the faith became incomprehensible to her. She couldn't read or concentrate. In her great hopelessness, Faustina felt that all of her personal striving for virtues or mortifications was pointless, as surely it had all become disagreeable to God. It was debilitating to even think about praying or doing good works.

Faustina tried to hide her suffering from her religious sisters, but her face betrayed her anguish. The sisters misinterpreted her. They thought she was pretending in order to be released from her religious duties. Her superiors were also unsure what to do with Faustina. They had already been reluctant to accept Faustina's reports of hearing or seeing Jesus, and this latest spiral downward only convinced them she was deluded. They did not recognize this as the true spiritual dark night it was and were unable to offer her help or consolation. All of this contributed to Faustina feeling further alienated and abandoned.

Faustina's faith staggered under such a fierce struggle. She clung to God—or at least her memory of God—by a sheer act of will, by blind obedience. It was the only path she could travel and her very last hope of survival. "In the midst of unspeakable torments, I imitated the blind man who entrusts himself to his guide, holding his hand firmly, not giving up obedience for a single moment, and this was my daily safety in this fiery trial" (*Divine Mercy in My Soul*, 68).

Although Faustina no longer felt worthy of the sacraments, her superiors and confessors ordered her to go to Confession and to receive Holy Communion, which proved to be good counsel. A few wise confessors could at least see that this suffering was a severe trial allowed by God and was earning great graces for the troubled sister. Her novice director at the time also counseled Faustina that she had been chosen for great sanctity and, therefore, to trust God with this trial; but none of this encouragement seemed to provide any lasting help.

During her struggles, Faustina made novenas to various saints for help, but nothing came of them. Then she recalled a saint that she was devoted to prior to entering religious life—St. Thérèse of Lisieux. Faustina decided to pray a novena to the Little Flower. On the fifth day of the novena, she dreamt St. Thérèse had come to her with a message. The great saint predicted that Faustina would also go to heaven and become a saint, but that she had to trust Jesus more in her trials.

Other than these occasional glimmers of hope, the cold darkness continued. At its worst, Faustina's dark night evoked within her soul a terrible hatred for all things holy. She was tormented by thoughts of being rejected by God and receiving the plight of the damned. At times, she felt she was the object of God's hatred and that her prayers would only anger God more. She was physically, emotionally, and spiritually exhausted; to her, death seemed the only way to end her suffering. In every sense of the word, Faustina felt complete abandonment by God.

On Good Friday in 1938, Faustina had a powerful spiritual experience; she felt the flames of divine love, and she came to understand how much Christ had suffered for his people. This experience increased her love and resolve and enabled her to continue her battle against spiritual darkness—a battle that would last another six months. At the conclusion of this time, she heard, "You are my joy; you are my heart's delight." After that, Faustina's soul was in intimate communion with God.

Professed Sister

Faustina survived her spiritual dark night and her time of novitiate. As a newly professed sister, she began to serve her congregation in many capacities and at many of the religious houses throughout Poland, but particularly at Kraków, Płock, and Vilnius (now part of Lithuania). This frequent moving from community to community worked in Faustina's favor because it allowed her keep her deep spiritual life hidden from her fellow sisters. Due to her lack of education, Faustina worked as a cook, gardener, baker, and doorkeeper in the different communities. She was enthusiastic in her duties, faithful in observing the rules of her order, recollected, silent, natural, cheerful, kind, and unselfish. To the other sisters, Faustina was nothing special; very few came to know that this young sister whom they considered so ordinary was, in reality, experiencing a rich interior life that would impact not only her, but, eventually, the lives of millions.

The young nun felt a responsibility to confide her experiences to her various superiors, but oftentimes they tried to dissuade her. Most could not accept that a human being could have such deep communion with God. Her claims of intimate union with the Lord earned her more disapproval and persecution than praise; she was often labeled as hysteric or eccentric. At times, Faustina was afraid of being deluded—as the others had accused her of being—and she tried to run from God, but he pursued his daughter nonetheless.

Faustina eventually found herself striving to live in even fuller union with God and melding her will with his. Her personal mission was to become a great saint by loving God more than any other person before her and to accomplish this through a self-sacrificing cooperation with Jesus to save souls. Her steadfast faithfulness to God was rewarded with many mystical gifts: contemplation, deep knowledge of the mystery of the mercy of God, visions, revelations, hidden stigmata, prophecy, reading of souls, and mystical espousal. Faustina had both physical and intellectual visions of Jesus in various forms. The Virgin Mary, angels, saints, and deceased souls visited her. She was shown heaven, purgatory, and hell, and even experienced a beatific vision in which she was snatched up before the very throne of God and saw the special place prepared for her in heaven. She had these mystical experiences not only in the privacy of her cell, but during Mass, adoration, and even while performing ordinary duties.

Growth in Holiness

Faustina understood that the supernatural gifts she was being given were a great grace, but that her sanctity still depended on working on and overcoming her faults. "Neither graces, nor revelations, nor raptures, nor gifts granted to a soul make it perfect, but rather the intimate vision of the soul with God . . . my sanctity and perfection is based upon the close union of my will with the will of God" (*Divine Mercy in My Soul*, 1107). Therefore, she worked daily toward spiritual perfection, even charting her daily victories and falls. Among the latter, she would list such things as breaking the rule of silence, not being obedient at the sound of the bell, and what she considered as meddling into people's affairs. Faustina had no trouble identifying her sins and confessing them to a priest. It was far more difficult for her to bare her extraordinary interior life with her confessors. She begged God to send her a spiritual director who could understand her soul, but he would be a long time coming.

In the meantime, Faustina learned to control her self-love and be truly humble before God. She strove for simplicity, humility, and a "spiritual childhood," much like the one modeled by St. Thérèse of Lisieux. She also learned to unite her sufferings, both physical and emotional, with the sacrifice of Jesus. Faustina spent a great deal of time meditating on Christ's passion and learning how the painful suffering of the Son of God constantly turns aside the wrath of God. She became willing to lay her life down for sinners, and once she had reached this point, God was ready to reveal to her the mission he had planned for her from the beginning: to be his messenger of mercy for the world.

Mission of Divine Mercy

Beginning in 1931, Faustina discovered she had been appointed by God to convey his message of mercy to the world:

> You are the secretary of my mercy; I have chosen you for that office in this and the next life . . . to make known to souls the great mercy I have for them, and to exhort them to trust in the bottomless depth of my mercy. (*Divine Mercy in My Soul*, 1605, 1567)

God let Faustina know that he did not wish to punish aching humankind, but wished to heal people, pressing them against his merciful heart.

The message of God's mercy was not a new one to the Church, as it can be found easily on the pages of holy scripture; but people seemed to have forgotten the transforming power of this mercy. Faustina reintroduced the world to God's healing mercy by presenting new devotions to it and thereby reviving spiritual life. As God told his daughter, before he comes as a just judge, he first comes as the king of mercy. He was granting the world a special period of time to employ this mercy in order to prepare it for his Second Coming. He wanted to inspire in people a trust in God's goodness and a living out of this mercy toward each neighbor through deed, word, and prayer.

Faustina learned that God's mercy can never be exhausted; he would not deny it to anyone who asks. He explained to her that when people place their trust in God, there is nothing to fear. The message of mercy is for all people, no matter their state of grace. In fact, it is the greatest message of hope for the most hardened sinners. As Faustina learned, the greater the sinner, the greater the right to God's mercy. "Let the greatest sinners place their trust in my mercy. They have the right before others to trust in the abyss of My mercy. . . . The more a soul trusts, the more mercy it will receive" (*Divine Mercy in My Soul*, 1146). He also cautioned Faustina, "Mankind will not have peace until it turns with trust to my mercy." These words were particularly relevant at a time when Faustina's country, Poland, was struggling for its independence and would soon fall victim to the rise of communism and Nazism.

Even greater than the evils of war is the evil of Satan, which Faustina also had to confront as she labored to carry out God's work. She learned that Satan hated mercy more than anything else. Mercy is his greatest torment because it rescues souls from falling into hell, which makes him furious. Therefore, he often tempted and threatened Faustina not to continue her work, but she ignored him and took shelter in Jesus' heart.

The Image

To inspire awareness of and participation in his mercy, Jesus presented Faustina with five elements of devotion to share with the world. The first was the image of the merciful Jesus. On February 22, 1931, Jesus appeared to Faustina in a white garment. One hand was raised in blessing and the other was touching his breast and slightly drawing aside his garment to reveal two rays of light—one red and the other white. As Faustina gazed upon the remarkable sight, she heard the words, "Paint an image according to the pattern you see, with the signature: Jesus, I trust in You. I desire that this image be venerated, first in your chapel, and [then] throughout the world" (*Divine Mercy in My Soul*, 327).

When Faustina shared this vision with her confessors and superiors, many told her it was an illusion. She was very conflicted over it. How could she carry out God's mission if no one would believe her? Finally her prayers for a spiritual director were answered. God showed her a vision of a priest who would eventually become her spiritual director and the visible help to carry out this important work. She met Father Michael Sopocko in 1933, shortly after making her perpetual vows. He was a professor at a university and seminary in Vilnius and occasionally would hear confessions at the Congregation of the Sisters of Our Lady of Mercy. When Father Sopocko first met Faustina, she told him she had seen him in a vision and he was chosen by God to help her carry out a divine plan. The priest disregarded her story at first and even had her tested by a psychiatrist. The psychiatrist maintained that she was mentally stable. After a while, Father Sopocko became intrigued with the sister's visions and spiritual insights. He remained her spiritual director until the end of her life. As she had predicted, he also became a great champion for the work of the Divine Mercy.

Father Sopocko urged Faustina to obtain a detailed meaning of the image she had seen. In answer, Jesus explained that the pale ray represents the water of Baptism that makes souls righteous. The red ray represents the blood that is the life of souls. "Happy is the one who will dwell in their shelter," he advised Faustina. He assured her that many graces would be granted to those who venerated this image. Convinced by this additional information and seeing that Faustina was unable to draw it herself, Father Sopocko commissioned artist Eugene Kazimeirowski to paint the image in 1934. Faustina was disappointed with the results and wept because it did not convey God's beauty. "Not in the beauty of the color, nor at the brush, lies the greatness of the image, but in my grace," Jesus reminded her to comfort her.

Feast of Divine Mercy

Jesus told Faustina he wanted the image to be solemnly blessed on the first Sunday after Easter, which he designated as the feast of Mercy. This, he told her, was a time of grace, a refuge and shelter for souls, especially poor sinners:

> Whoever approaches the Fount of Life on this day will be granted complete remission of sins and punishment. On this day, the very depths of my tender mercy are open. I pour out a whole ocean of graces upon those souls who approach the fount of my mercy . . . let no soul fear to draw near to me, even though his sins may be as scarlet. (*Divine Mercy in My Soul*, 300, 699)

The Chaplet of Divine Mercy

Jesus taught Faustina a prayer to be said on ordinary rosary beads. He called it the Chaplet of Divine Mercy (see appendix 2). It is to be said for the atonement of personal sin, sins of loved ones, and sins of the whole world. By reciting the words of this prayer, a person unites him- or herself with the sacrifice of Jesus. Praying the Chaplet of Divine Mercy is a way to appeal to God's compassion by asking his mercy on the world in consideration of Jesus' sorrowful passion. The chaplet is particularly effective when said for the dying, as it is the last hope of salvation for sinners. To pray the chaplet is considered a work of mercy. "Even the most hardened sinner need only to recite it once to receive grace from my infinite mercy," Jesus told Faustina.

The Novena

Jesus instructed Faustina that the best way to prepare for the feast of Mercy was to pray the Chaplet of Divine Mercy for nine consecutive days, called a novena. "By this novena I will grant every possible grace to souls," he told her.

The Hour of Mercy

Finally, Jesus also told Faustina that three o'clock in the afternoon was the Hour of Mercy. It was the hour he died on the cross for the sins of all and the moment when mercy was opened wide for every soul. He told her that God's mercy was especially available during this hour, every day, and that it was particularly pleasing for people to meditate on the Stations of the Cross during this hour, or at least pause and remember his great sacrifice.

Spreading the Devotion

Jesus promised Faustina that just as a tender mother shields her infant, he would shield those souls who practiced mercy and spread devotion to his divine mercy. At the hour of their death, he promised that he would be their merciful Savior, not a judge. His instructions on living out mercy toward one another were clear: "You are to show mercy to your neighbors always and everywhere. You must not shrink from this or try to excuse or absolve yourself from it. Practice at least one act of love of neighbor each day."

Renewal of Religious Life

Jesus desired religious orders to be renewed in love and obedience to his will. He also desired a new congregation to be formed that would proclaim the mercy of God to the world and, by its prayers, obtain mercy for the world. Faustina felt a strong urge to start this congregation herself, even to the point of being tempted to leave her current congregation to take this action; but her confessors and superiors cautioned her to proceed slowly. At times, she grew agitated and frustrated, wanting to go to the Holy Father himself in Rome about the new congregation and the Divine Mercy in general; but Father Sopocko wisely advised against it, saying it would be more harmful than helpful at that point. His instinct was that the devotion should begin in Poland with the cooperation of bishops and archbishops, before petitioning the Holy Father for a worldwide devotion. The times were dangerous in Europe and he wanted to move with extreme caution. Obedient to her confessor, Faustina took no further action. She foresaw that there would be a male and a female congregation, as well as a huge association of lay people to promulgate the message of mercy, but that this would not occur in her lifetime. (In fact, she was correct. The Congregation of the Most Holy Lord Jesus Christ, Merciful Redeemer, was established in 1955.)

The Diary

Father Sopocko provided the sound spiritual guidance Faustina needed for the mission God had entrusted her. Because he was unable to listen to her lengthy confessions, the astute priest ordered Faustina to begin a diary to record the visions and messages she had received and was continuing to receive. Faustina obeyed and wrote notes in a series of notebooks during the last four years of her life. At one

time, Faustina believed that an angel had told her to burn
her notes. She did, but Father Sopocko, seeing that she had
been deceived, ordered her to recreate the missing sections.
Faustina did this while continuing to add new revelations,
which is why her diary is not in chronological order. Still, the
diary reflects the high degree of union with God as well as
her efforts and struggles on the way to Christian perfection.
The light she has shed on the mystical life of the soul and her
unparalleled understanding of God's divine mercy have led
many scholars to consider her diary, *Divine Mercy in My Soul*,
as one of the most important spiritual works of literature in
the two-thousand-year history of the Church.

An Eternal Mission

Like Thérèse, Faustina seemed to have a growing awareness
that the work to which God had called her would be continued after her death.

> Poor earth, I will not forget you. Although I feel that I will
> be immediately drowned in God as in an ocean of happi-
> ness, that will not be an obstacle to my returning to earth
> to encourage souls and incite them to trust in God's mercy.
> (*Divine Mercy in My Soul*, 1582)

She had a premonition about the writings in her diary
and her intercession in the lives of many. She prayed a novena
to St. Frances Xavier, the great missionary saint, for the grace
to do good after her death and felt certain her request would
be granted. Toward the end of her life, she seemed to know
that her body would not be preserved, but that people would
be looking for her relics. She spoke of letters the sisters would
receive after her death—letters that would bring them joy.
She knew she would be a model for ordinary people, for
"little souls," teaching them her ordinary way of trust and
surrender.

Also like Thérèse, Faustina battled tuberculosis. In her case, the deadly diseased attacked her lungs and digestive system, and her physical suffering increased in intensity with each passing month. She finally succumbed to this disease on October 5, 1938, at the age of thirty-three and in her thirteenth year of religious life. Though the disease had left her emaciated and twisted in pain, her final moment on earth was one of peace as she raised her eyes toward heaven and her body took on an unearthly beauty. Two days later, a small, simple funeral was held with no family present. Faustina had wanted to spare them grief and travel expenses and had requested that the community not notify them about her terminal illness or death.

For the most part, Faustina died in obscurity. Few in her communities had known of her extraordinary mystical experiences, and even fewer had believed in them. The sisters who lived and worked with Faustina were familiar with the Divine Mercy prayer and image because the congregation had been circulating them for a few years, but none of them knew that Faustina had been the messenger. It wasn't until two years after her death that her name began to be publically linked with the devotion, and the mother general visited all the religious houses in the order to give the sisters the full story of Faustina's special mission. Needless to say, the sisters were astonished.

A Message of Hope for the World

More than anything else, the message of Divine Mercy that Faustina received from Jesus was (and is) a message of hope. Perhaps it is only fitting, therefore, that the messenger Jesus selected for this mission was a woman who exhibited heroic degrees of the virtue of hope during her short spiritual journey on earth. Faustina put her hope in the fact that her visions and messages were not delusions, but genuine intercessions of the God she adored. In the face of skepticism, poor spiritual counsel, and even a deep and prolonged interior darkness, the young nun clung to the hope that the sun would never go out, no matter how thick and slow-moving the clouds; and she endured each challenge willingly for the salvation of souls. Faustina had learned to trust God without limit and with her very life. "My only hope is in you," she proclaimed to Jesus in her writings.

Perhaps it was also fitting that the seeds of the Divine Mercy Devotion were planted in Poland, a predominantly Catholic country where Catholicism has long been a part of the Polish identity. The nation's strong Catholic faith and culture have historically separated it from its bordering neighbors. This faith played a key role in Poland's fight for independence and national survival. At the time Faustina was writing in her diary, her beloved country, like so many nations in Europe, was losing sight of hope in the shadow of the evil that was pervading the continent. Hardly a year after her death, Adolf Hitler's army invaded Poland and defeated the Polish army in three weeks. For the millions who were oppressed, tortured, and put to death under this terrible regime, hope seemed all but lost. The Divine Mercy devotion became a shield of strength and hope for many in Poland and throughout all of Europe, but this did not come without cost.

Satan was not happy with the spread of this message of mercy. He did not want lukewarm and particularly grave sinners to regain their hope and confidence in God's unfathomable mercy. For the prince of darkness, this meant the risk of losing a great number of souls that would have been destined to eternal damnation. The feast day on the Sunday after Easter, in which Jesus promised the absolution of sin and its temporal effects, was like a second Baptism for sinners. The hope, like the mercy, was unfathomable; and Satan was bent on silencing this message once and for all.

Challenges to the Devotion

Faustina had predicted correctly in 1935 that the devotion to divine mercy would be met with adversity: "There will come a time when this work, which God is demanding so very much, will be as though utterly undone. And then God will act with great power, which will give evidence of its authority" (*Divine Mercy in My Soul*, 378). She foresaw the feast day being celebrated in Rome as well as her convent chapel, but she knew before that day would come, there would be days of struggle and strife.

Her spiritual director, Father Michael Sopocko, experienced these challenges firsthand. As Faustina also foresaw, this courageous priest would suffer obstacles, persecution, ridicule, and rejection because of his work as a zealous apostle for the Divine Mercy Devotion. He risked his very life to smuggle copies of the image, the prayer, and Faustina's writings within communist Poland. Devotion spread throughout the small nation almost spontaneously because this message of mercy was greatly needed for the war-torn nation. He was also instrumental in getting the message to the rest of Europe and the outside world. He tirelessly worked to advance its cause for gaining Church approval.

The rapid spreading of the devotion to the divine mercy was halted, however, when erroneous and confusing translations of Faustina's diary made their way to the Vatican. Because of the delicate political situation in Communist Poland, it was difficult for the Church to authenticate Faustina's writings. Therefore, in 1958, the Holy See made the decision to ban devotion to the Divine Mercy, just as Faustina had foretold.

Images were removed from their places of veneration and circulation of materials ceased. Roman officials severely admonished Father Sopocko, and it looked as if the work was completely destroyed. One glimmer of hope remained, however. The archbishop of Kraków gave permission for the Sisters of Mercy to keep the original image in their chapel at Lagiewniki, where Faustina's body lay in the cemetery. Here, a flicker of the devotion continued.

Triumph of Mercy

Thirty-seven years after Faustina's death, the archbishop of Kraków, Karol Wojtyla (the future Pope John Paul II), began a formal investigation into the life of Sister Maria Faustina. As a young priest, he had been exposed to the Divine Mercy Devotion and recognized the powerful and timely message of hope it offered the world. He also had access to many of the original documents that the Holy See did not have in 1958. Father Michael Sopocko lived long enough to testify to Faustina's heroic virtues for the purposes of this investigation. He died with the hope that worldwide devotion to the Divine Mercy would eventually come to fruition.

In 1978, the Sacred Congregation for the Doctrine of the Faith, after studying the results of the investigation, lifted the 1958 ban on Divine Mercy. Once again, the faithful were permitted to venerate the Divine Mercy image, pray the Chaplet, and read Faustina's diary, which was quickly translated into multiple languages. Six months later, Cardinal Wojtyla was elected pope. The influence of Divine Mercy was evident in the new pontiff, as his second encyclical is titled *Dives in Misericordia* (Rich in Mercy). Pope John Paul II's work to promulgate the message of mercy was not finished, however. He beatified Faustina in 1993 and gave Polish bishops permission to celebrate the Feast of Divine Mercy in 1995 (which he concurrently celebrated in Rome). For the occasion of the ever-important Jubilee year of 2000, he solemnly canonized Faustina as the first saint of the third millennium, referring to her as the Apostle of Divine Mercy and the great apostle of the twentieth century. He also established the feast of Mercy throughout the entire Church and entrusted the world to this mercy.

Mercy Today

St. Faustina's life, mission, and writings have sparked a great grassroots movement within the Catholic Church. This simple and uneducated Polish nun and the bold mission she recorded from the Master's mouth have inspired millions to turn their lives over to God with childlike trust. The gift of God's mercy, dormant within the Church for a long time, has been rekindled in a powerful new way to make it accessible for all—particularly great sinners. It is an attitude and a way of life that illumines a path for people of the third millennium to recall and embrace God's mercy in their own lives and look for opportunities to extend this loving mercy toward their neighbor. Millions have echoed the words of Faustina with great hope in their hearts: "Jesus I love you. Jesus, I trust in you."

While Jesus' words to Faustina in the years preceding World War II certainly brought hope to the world at one of its darkest times in history, I can't help but wonder if Jesus didn't have our times in mind when he gave Faustina those messages. Surely he would have foreseen the darkness we contend with today in the forms of aggressive secularism, immorality, disregard for life, war, terrorism, and corruption. In his wisdom, he knew that, once again, hope in his mercy is the balm we would need. Hope is a belief in a good outcome. It is not wishful thinking, but an active participation in that outcome through the means of prayer and acts of good will.

As human beings, we need hope. We cannot live without it. It is such a powerful state of mind that it has been shown to alter the neurochemistry of the brain to produce psychologically positive effects.

Of all the messages Jesus gave Faustina to share with the world, I can think of none more hopeful than the promise he imparted to her about Divine Mercy Sunday. On Divine Mercy Sunday he would pour out his mercy, giving us, in essence, a direct entry into eternal life in heaven through the complete washing away of all sin and its temporal effects. What an amazing promise! Will people today and in the future respond to that message? One can only hope.

LESSONS IN HOPE
FROM FAUSTINA

The tangible "ocean of mercy" I felt after leaving the confessional that day back in the 1990s made Jesus' words through Faustina take on new meaning for me in a powerful way. It was a transforming experience to know I was truly forgiven for what I had deemed unforgivable. Although I haven't experienced the same tangible sensation since the day of that great miracle, I know that every time I make a sincere confession in which I am honest about my sinfulness and firmly resolved to try harder, I am washed clean by God's mercy and invited to start over. Every time anyone approaches the Lord of forgiveness in that manner, he or she receives that great gift and promise to be unburdened and permitted to begin anew. This special experience has liberated me from my negative thoughts about the sacrament. I no longer drag my feet, dreading when it is time to make a confession. It's not that Confession is easy; it's not supposed to be. The process of admitting our faults in front of another human being, especially a representative of the Church, should make us squirm a bit and feel remorseful. If it doesn't, it might mean we are not digging down deep enough. I have to question myself often if there isn't something other than the same short list of offenses I typically bring into the confessional time after time. I try and remember to ask the Holy Spirit to enlighten my heart and mind to what it is I most need to confess on a given day. Sometimes these prayers can reveal surprising answers. The important thing is that now I know with confidence who awaits me in that confessional; it is Jesus with open arms, ready to give me his forgiveness and unconditional love, despite my failings. That gives me the courage to be more vulnerable and honest in admitting my faults. Today, I find that confessing twice a year is no longer enough for me; every other month or even monthly feels more appropriate.

My renewed appreciation of the Sacrament of Reconciliation and the realization that I had been given a tremendous unmerited grace prompted me to share the story in a magazine article titled "Confessions of a Catholic Convert," which ran in *St. Anthony Messenger* in 2003. It took fortitude and a lot of prayer for me to expose myself like that, but I decided that God had graced me so that I could help others. Almost immediately after the article ran, a woman contacted me to thank me for my sharing. She told me she had always struggled with the Sacrament of Reconciliation, but reading the article gave her the courage to go back after twenty years of being away.

That was all the confirmation I needed to see the hand of God at work. Only he could take such a dark situation in my life and use it to bring light to others. In that sense, it was all worth it. Since that article, I've spoken on what I call the joy of Reconciliation to many audiences. I've addressed small children ready to receive this sacrament for the first time. They are naturally filled with curiosity, but also a lot of anxiety. Many of their parents don't use this sacrament regularly because of misunderstandings and even hurts associated with confession, and these negative emotions often filter down to their children. When students hear the way God allowed me to "feel" his mercy that day, they are no longer afraid and have told me so in many precious thank-you letters afterward. They are now eager to receive God's mercy.

I once gave my talk on Reconciliation as part of a women's retreat in northern Ohio. I spoke on Faustina and the Divine Mercy message first, which was a perfect topic since it was the season of Lent. The women were very receptive to the story of this simple Polish nun and her message of God's love and forgiveness for the world. I followed that presentation with one on confession and my discovery of the gift and graces of this often-forgotten sacrament. Before the closing Mass, there was an opportunity for the women to receive the Sacrament of Reconciliation. There were so many women in line at the confessionals that they had to bring in the retired bishop of Cleveland to help administer the sacrament. These women heard and responded to the invitation of Jesus himself, gently calling them to release the burdens they had been carrying in their hearts (some for many years) that they had been afraid to let go. As I was leaving the closing Mass, the pastor grabbed me by the arm. He was as excited as a little kid on Christmas morning. He asked if I had seen the long lines for confession. I acknowledged that the Holy Spirit certainly seemed to be at work that day. With a beaming smile, he whispered that one of the women he had met with had been away from the sacrament for forty years. When I hear stories like that, my heart is filled with hope that with God, all things are possible. Healed hearts, changed lives, new beginnings, the discovery of joy—all of this can happen when we put our trust in Jesus and his unfathomable love and mercy.

Jesus, I Trust in You

When Jesus appeared to Faustina in the cell of her convent, he showed himself with his hand raised in blessing and red and white rays issuing from his heart. He explained to her that these rays represent the blood and water poured forth for the world when a lance pierced his agonizing heart as he was on the cross. He was very clear with Faustina that he desired for this image to be venerated throughout the world. It was, he explained, a vessel of great graces and a fountain of his mercy. All who would venerate this image would not perish; he himself would defend them at their hour of death.

Jesus instructed Faustina to mark the image with this signature: "Jesus, I Trust in You." While several versions of the image have been created since the original one was painted in Poland, all are marked with these important words. Regardless of the actual image, each is a vehicle of God's grace when revered with trust in his mercy.

I've always loved the Divine Mercy image. It is not uncommon for me to have holy cards with this image taped to my computer or stuck in the pages of my Bible. Looking at Jesus and those rays of light emitting from his heart always brings me a sense of comfort. The last words I utter in my nighttime prayers are, "Jesus I love you. Jesus, I trust in you." For years, I said these words with contentment and confidence. Of course I loved Jesus. Of course I trusted him. What was not to trust? Soon, I would be tested though; and Jesus and Faustina helped me to have a much better understanding of what true trust is all about.

Father Samuel

Someone who has been very instrumental in my faith walk (and that of my husband) is a priest named Father Samuel. We first met this white-haired, white-bearded man in black on a trip to Nashville, Tennessee, to see our friends' daughter make her first profession as a Dominican of the Congregation of St. Cecilia, commonly known as the Nashville Dominicans. On the way down, my husband and I got into a terrible fight. We could not seem to reach healing and forgiveness, even with the intervention of a family Rosary. We arrived at Nashville not speaking to each other and filled with anger and hurt in our hearts. At a small reception in the hotel, we were introduced to a priest named Samuel who had a smile on his lips and a twinkle in his eye. Father Samuel was the father of ten and grandfather of twenty-one! I remember my brain trying to wrap itself around that reality. We learned that Father Samuel was a late-life vocation. His wife had died of ovarian cancer some years back, and he had recently been ordained as a priest of the Institute of the Incarnate Word. We politely greeted him, but because of our argument, neither of us felt very sociable. Later on, when the reception had begun to thin out as people retired to their bedrooms, Father Samuel returned to the hospitality room to pick up his breviary that he had inadvertently left behind. He took one look at the two of us with our unhappy faces and sat down with a wink and a mischievous look. I knew instantly that God had sent this man to help heal us, even though, in my pride, I had no intention of reconciling with my husband. It only took a few minutes of small talk, however, before my tears betrayed my pent-up emotions, and I confessed that the two of us had been struggling. Father Samuel offered to hear our confessions, and that was just what we needed to finally heal our hardened hearts.

It has become quite clear to both my husband and me that Father Samuel is like a guardian angel and spiritual director sent to us by God. I think that my first spiritual companion, Thérèse, also had something to do with it. It happened that two weeks before he met me, Father had read my book about Thérèse, *Shower of Heavenly Roses: Stories of the Intercession of St. Thérèse of Lisieux*. He told me later that the book had inspired him to pray a novena to the Little Flower. He didn't specify an intention for the novena, however. He simply told Thérèse to use it for whatever cause she desired. Father believes the novena is what brought the three of us together. In any case, whenever my husband and I are struggling, Father Samuel "happens" to call. He's always there with the right words that give us the clarity we need. His advice, at times, has been challenging, even rocking us to the core; but each time we've clung to the words, "Jesus I trust in you" and with God's grace we have been able to act on his advice.

Giving God His Due

One particularly challenging area that Father Samuel lovingly guided us through was the subject of tithing a full ten percent as prescribed in the Old Testament. I don't remember exactly how that subject came up; perhaps we were talking about financial concerns. Father is not one to lecture or admonish. He gently shares himself, and our hearts are moved just by listening. He told us of the days when his wife and he had eight or nine children and he was between jobs. He heard a talk by a man who spoke of the importance of tithing the full ten percent, like it says in the Old Testament. After the talk, Father was inspired to put his last five dollar bill into the collection basket. There were many times he and his wife wondered how they would feed their children, but somehow God always provided. It came through anonymous envelopes of money put in their mailbox, or friends calling to see if they could use an old car. Through these generous and timely gestures, they paid their bills, put food on the table, and survived. God was always faithful.

Listening to his story, both Mark and I were moved to reevaluate our own mentality about giving back to the Church or other charitable causes. We were probably tithing about four or five percent of our income then, but we felt justified that the time and talent we shared in the many ministries we performed more than made up for the difference. After all, our time was valuable, and we did have four mouths to feed. Certainly God wouldn't want us denying their basic needs. The more we prayed after that phone conversation with Father, though, the more we realized God was asking us to trust him with our finances. So, the first of the month came, and, as the one who pays the bills, I calculated what we had earned the previous month. When I figured ten percent of that, my jaw dropped. God couldn't be asking that we part with that much money a month—it was more than a car payment! We simply couldn't afford it. I grew panicky and nauseated just thinking about it. But there was this persistent feeling that wouldn't go away. This was what we were supposed to do, as uncomfortable as it felt. "Jesus, I trust in you. Jesus I trust in you." The words reverberated in my head as I wrote a check to our parish, knowing our pastor would be quite surprised. Somehow the other bills got paid that month and life went on.

The process of tithing gradually grew easier for us, but it took some time. A turning point for me was when I began to think of the money as God's money, and it actually became kind of fun, calculating the amount each month and asking him where he wanted his gift to go this time. There was never a shortage of need—friends who had a house fire, another who lost his job, a natural disaster, school debt for someone wanting to enter religious life—each month there was always a perfect opportunity to share God's generosity with others. If questioned about it, we told people that we had come to trust in God that he would provide for us if we helped to provide for others. Many of our friends and family members were inspired to begin tithing, too. The ironic thing for me is that writing those big checks back in those days seemed hard enough, but it would become far more difficult to write small checks when our financial situation took a serious turn for the worse. Still, we've been faithful to the ten-percent promise, and God continues to be faithful to his.

Fertility

Father Samuel also helped us with was our fertility. All our married life, Mark and I had used Natural Family Planning as a means to achieve or postpone pregnancy. We learned how to deal with the necessary times of abstinence each month, which wasn't always easy, and we welcomed the times of pregnancy or breastfeeding, when fertility was deferred and we had a bit more flexibility in our lovemaking. Once we were in our forties and content that our family was complete, we longed for the time when I would no longer be fertile so we could enjoy spontaneous encounters without fear or anxiety. The situation was becoming increasingly difficult, especially for my husband. Nonetheless, my body showed no sign of slowing down from having regular cycles. It wasn't long before I began resenting my fertility and even talked about doing something about it, but we would always return to the reality that neither one of us would be happy with that decision. We knew in our hearts it would be wrong. So we continued to struggle and prayed that God would give us an answer.

One Saturday morning as we lay in bed bemoaning our situation, the phone rang. To no surprise, it was Father

Samuel. We shared with him our dilemma, figuring he could especially relate as a previously married man. Father listened patiently, as he always did. We both expected him to tell Mark to back off and be patient. To both our surprise, he addressed me. With love and compassion, he reminded me that God would not give me something I couldn't handle. I needed to trust God and be open to my husband. I began to shake, literally. What was Father saying? Didn't he realize I was forty-seven years old and it was dangerous for me to have a child at my age? What about the danger to the child—how could we possibly bring a baby with a disability into the world? What about our other children? How would they be affected? As he often did, Father told us to open the scriptures. First, he had us read about Abraham and his yes to God, even to the possibility of sacrificing his only son. Then he had us read about Mary and her yes to God, even to the possibility of scorn and rejection by Joseph and her family, friends, and community. I obediently read these stories, but I was not Abraham or Mary. I was me, and I was scared to death at the possibility of letting go and trusting God in this area of my life. Anything but this Lord, I thought, anything but this. I cried. I begged. Mark cried too. He was also scared. Trusting God in this area was unequivocally the single hardest decision I've ever had to make in my life. This was the ultimate letting-go-of-the-branch moment for me. I was sure that by turning my fertility over to God my life was over.

I think it took a while, and it wasn't without a great deal of reluctance, but I began to let go of control. I had to fight hard not to blame Mark for this. I knew this was a turning point in my walk of faith—God and Faustina were standing before me asking me how much I trusted. Could I surrender what felt like was my entire life and future? Like a person closing his eyes and making that decision to jump out of a plane despite the terror within, I leapt. Each month when my period would return on schedule, I prayed with heartfelt thanksgiving that I had not conceived. Month after month, it was the same. It was a long time before I would stop calculating the days in my head as to where I was in my cycle and finally let go of my anxiety.

Years later, it has become clear to the two of us what God was trying to teach us through this challenging situation. He was aware of our faithfulness and our desire for one another, and he wanted to bless us. He wanted to gift us with spontaneity in our relationship, but in order to receive that gift we had to open our hands to accept it. We had to let go of the fear and anxiety I especially had been clinging desperately to. Had we not trusted that God knew what was best for us, we would have missed out on years of free and joyful expressions of love. It has been wonderfully freeing for me in particular to no longer live in fear and anxiety in this area of our life. This situation has made me realize that I spent too many years of my marriage in that state of mind, much to the detriment of both of us. By trusting fully in God with the help of Faustina, we have helped our love and marriage blossom into something more beautiful than either of us could have ever imagined.

The scripture verses that Father Samuel had us reflect on during that struggle also shed some important light for us. Sometimes God asks for our yes and the willingness to change our lives in an instant. He did that with Mary when he accepted and acted on her yes and gave her a son who would change the world. Other times though, God asks for our yes just to hear us say it, just as he did with Abraham. Abraham was ready to climb the hill of sacrifice and see it to the end, until God delivered him from sacrificing his son, Isaac. It was a test, but not for God. God already knew Abraham's heart. The test was for Abraham so he could see for himself how much he loved and trusted God and how loving and merciful God is in return.

On a Hopeful Note

Faustina introduced me to God's mercy. She taught me what it means to trust God and how beautiful results happen when you do. She continues to be there for me every time life demands that I trust in Jesus (which is quite often), and I use her example of steadfast hope that God is in charge and knows what he is doing at all times.

What most impresses me is that, even in her darkest night, Faustina retained the hope that God would not abandon her. Through her I have come to see that God uses all situations in life, both good and bad, to accomplish his plans. I have also learned how hope is the strongest weapon against Satan. The evil one tempted Faustina as he tempts us with discouragement, his chief weapon, to make us less effective warriors and shut us down from doing God's work. But each time Faustina clung to God, whom she fully trusted; and Satan was rendered powerless. When I am feeling discouraged and tempted to despair, I ask Faustina for her intercession. I know that just uttering the words, "Jesus I trust in you," even when I don't genuinely feel it, can cause the devil to flee. His weapon may be discouragement, but ours is hope, and that is always the stronger weapon.

Pope Emeritus Benedict XVI recognized the importance of this spiritual weapon. He devoted an entire encyclical to the virtue of hope and its importance in the world today. In *Spe Savli* (Saved in Hope), he writes that to really know God, we must have hope. It is what defines us as Christians. As the Holy Father explains, those of us who believe know that our lives will not end in emptiness. We have a future. Many people in the world, however, live in darkness, without God and without hope, and this is a tragedy. For the Christian who has hope, the future is certain and the present therefore can be lived well. Hope gives meaning and purpose to our journeys. As a result, we live our lives differently because of this hope. Hope grants us new life because it is a gift that changes the life of those who receive it. To have true hope, it is necessary first to have faith, which is the final virtue we address in this book. This virtue was taught best to me by my third spiritual journey partner, St. Bernadette Soubirous.

Where Healing
Waters Flow

I first became aware of St. Bernadette Soubirous when I was reading about famous Catholic apparitions during my early years in the faith. In those days, the concept of the Virgin Mary appearing to select individuals—often children—was more intriguing to me than the actual visionaries themselves. The story of Lourdes in particular sounded a bit like a children's fairy tale, with a charming character named Bernadette who, as a young teen in a cave in the hills of southern France, encountered the Virgin. I didn't feel particularly drawn to the story or retain much of its details, except that it had something to do with "magic water" that healed people of their ailments and continued to attract pilgrims in modern times. This part of the story bordered on superstitious Catholicism for me, and I was dissuaded from looking into it any further.

I'm surprised, as I think about it now, that I have no recollection of seeing the movie, *The Song of Bernadette*, which earned Jennifer Jones an Academy Award for her portrayal of the fourteen-year-old French visionary. Our family thoroughly enjoyed watching old movies on television, and I was quite familiar with many Hollywood actors from the silver screen, but somehow this particular piece of cinema never made it into my childhood bank of Catholic entertainment. Perhaps if it did, I might have had a better attitude about it.

A Special Writing Assignment

My attitudes about the apparitions of Bernadette changed, however, when one of my publishers called me in 2006 to ask if I would consider writing a book on Lourdes to commemorate its upcoming 150th anniversary. At first, I felt honored and enthusiastic about the prospect of working on what sounded like a terrific project. Then doubts began to settle in. I knew I could do general research to tell the story of this young girl and her eighteen apparitions, but that wouldn't be the same as actually going there and experiencing the shrine for myself. With four boys in tow and finances tight, it didn't seem likely that I was going to be able to jump on a plane and fly across the ocean to get some firsthand information for the book. I also wasn't sure what I could say about Lourdes that would be new or exciting. My impression was that so much had been written on those apparitions already. What could I possibly add that would be relevant?

I told my editor I would pray about it and discuss it with my husband. Mark is always a good sounding board for me when I'm discerning new projects. The two of us were on our way to the wooded hills of southeastern Ohio to seek some much needed rest and relaxation. As we bubbled in the hot tub on the back deck of our cabin, we talked about the idea of going to a faraway place like Lourdes and walking in the footsteps of Bernadette. It sounded so exciting, yet so preposterous. When we returned home, I decided to ask God for a clear indication about whether or not I should take on this project. I had already had my heart set on another book idea, and I needed to know for certain if this was a direction or a distraction. To try and find answers, I began to poke around a little bit on the Internet to see what I could learn about this remote village in southern France.

To my great surprise, I discovered that Lourdes was making newspaper headlines around the world. It seemed that the town's bishop and medical director were petitioning Rome about a plan to revise the traditional method of reporting, analyzing, and documenting inexplicable cures that are widely associated with Lourdes. I learned that the rapid advance of medicine and diagnostics was making it increasingly difficult to adhere to the criteria that had been established in the 1700s for the Church to verify miracles. This explained why there were only sixty-seven cures officially approved as miraculous by Rome, despite the fact that six million pilgrims travel to Lourdes each year and stories abound of physical, spiritual, and emotional healings. I thought this development sounded particularly newsworthy, and it was the impetus for me to take on the project.

Pilgrim and Journalist

Still, there was the matter of getting to France. I had no choice but to turn the situation over to God and let him work out those details. My husband and I decided to update our passports, just in case. We figured that if God were going to open some doors, we needed to be prepared to walk through them. Meanwhile, I continued my research. It wasn't long before I came across Marlene Watkins, the founder of Our Lady of Lourdes Hospitality North American Volunteers. She is a woman who experienced a life-changing personal healing while being submersed in the waters of the baths at Lourdes. Marlene claims she was given a special grace to bring others to the sanctuary: those in need of healing and those to serve those who seek the grace of Lourdes. I phoned Marlene, and when she heard that an American author was interested in writing a new book on Lourdes for the upcoming anniversary, she became an instant advocate. She informed me that there were actually far fewer books about the apparitions written in English than in other languages. The bigger problem, she explained, was that the narratives were often flawed, with story-like embellishments as a result of fictional books and movies made about Bernadette and her visions. Marlene was anxious to see an accurate and up-to-date telling of the story for an English-speaking audience.

Marlene was instrumental in making it possible for Mark and me to join her on an October pilgrimage to Lourdes that consisted of both volunteers and people with disabilities. We would get to meet those who served and those who came to be served at the shrine. It was the perfect answer to our prayers. She arranged for me to work closely with one of the world's leading living authorities on Lourdes, Father Régis-Marie de la Teyssonnière, who had served at the sanctuary as spiritual director for over a decade. Father Régis-Marie graciously agreed to review my manuscript to prevent any errors from creeping into my writing. His sole trusted authority on the subject of Lourdes was the world-renowned Marian theologian Father René Laurentin, who had authored no less than thirty volumes on Bernadette and her apparitions. Father Régis-Marie immediately pointed me to what he felt was the most accurate characterization of the French saint: *Bernadette Speaks: A Life of Saint Bernadette Soubirous in Her Own Words* by Father Laurentin. It was this impressive volume, along with Patricia McEachern's *A Holy Life: The Writings of St. Bernadette of Lourdes* that made Bernadette—the real Bernadette—move off the pages of a fairy tale and assume the role of a serious spiritual mentor and spiritual journey partner in my life.

In addition to his expertise on the history of Lourdes, the multilingual Father Régis-Marie was also well connected at the sanctuary. He arranged for me to have private interviews with key people throughout the shrine for an inside look at this major center of spiritualty today. Many of these interviews required translators, which he also arranged for me. Between Marlene and Father, I was able to meet with the bishop, the rector, the general chaplain, the medical director, the former president of hospitality, the international hospitality coordinator, the communications director, numerous chaplains, and veteran volunteers. Each gave me a glimpse into the past, present, and future of this important Marian site of apparition.

It was a bit challenging for me that week to constantly switch hats from playing the role of investigative journalist one moment to simple pilgrim the next, trying to absorb the marvelous sights and sounds of this international place of worship. I found Lourdes to be beautiful—its picturesque castle-like main basilica is perched on the River Gave and cradled by the Pyrenees Mountains of southern France. I was pleased to see the sanctuary grounds preserved as a place of holiness, at least inside the gates of the property. Outside the wrought-iron perimeter, hotels and restaurants and an endless stream of souvenir shops squeeze into every inch of the surrounding hilly streets, hoping to lure pilgrims with their wares and services. Within the sanctuary walls there are beautiful churches, statues, promenades, and outdoor places of prayer that inspire peace and holiness. None accomplished this atmosphere more than the grotto itself. It is truly the heart of the sanctuary, the place where it all started, the hallowed spot where heaven and earth had once united, and the reason that each pilgrim had come. The impact of kneeling on the pavement before that sheer-rock wall and the niche with the smiling statue of Our Lady looking down at us is hard to describe in words, even for a writer.

Personal Miracles

People have often asked me if I had experienced any miracles while I was in Lourdes. For me, the whole trip was a miracle. The evidence of God's hand at work from the start was as clear to me as the crystal water of the miraculous spring. From the timing of the pilgrimage, to the people we were graced to travel with, to the invaluable connections I was able to make while there—everything about the pilgrimage was grace and blessing. There were a number of powerful spiritual moments during our precious days at Lourdes. For example, I was able to make an important Confession there to unburden something from my childhood that had surprisingly surfaced in my consciousness just before our trip. We participated in a deeply moving Mass at the home of Bernadette and experienced the humbling and profoundly peace-filled phenomenon of being submersed in the baths. Mark and I were also afforded some special privileges during our pilgrimage. He was able to work in the baths one of the days we were there, and we both were asked to lead a portion of the Rosary to a candle-bearing sea of humanity during the torchlight procession. That was an experience I will never forget.

One of my most memorable moments at Lourdes, however, was the afternoon I was able to spend some quiet time at the grotto. Contained in the inner pockets of my backpack was a computer-generated document of prayer petitions we had received prior to departing for France. We had cut and pasted these petitions hastily into one document, not reading them beforehand, but assuring the senders we would take them and pray them at Lourdes. For a solid hour on my knees, I prayed those prayers and supplications under the gaze of the Virgin from the niche above. There were prayers for individual causes and prayers for the world at large. There were requests for healing from illness and heartbreaking pleas to the Virgin for lost children to return to the faith. There were prayers for employment, forgiveness, fertility, and increased faith. There were also prayers of thanksgiving for an equally diverse list of reasons.

It was touching for me to witness the faith of these people and the vulnerable way they had trusted their deepest hurts and longings with us in these petitions. Tearfully I prayed each petition slowly and with as much reverence as I could. As I prayed, I felt a strong sense that these prayers were being heard. They were not just my prayers, either, but those of the many pilgrims around me, engrossed in their own silent conversations. The grotto was holy ground. The Blessed Mother's presence could still be felt in this place. I could not see her with my eyes as Bernadette was privileged to a century and a half ago, but I could certainly feel her with my heart.

Faith in Action

Praying those petitions in the grotto really brought home the message of Lourdes to me. That experience allowed me to glimpse into the inner recesses of people's hearts and witness the great faith they had in the Virgin and her son. Such conviction is what has prompted millions of pilgrims across time and miles to travel to the very spot in which I was kneeling. I recalled from my research how many of the pilgrims with illness and disability, particularly in the early years, perished on the long and arduous journey to Lourdes. They came despite the risk, with faith that their situation might be improved. Perhaps they, too, would find an astonishing cure and be able to add their crutches to the dozens that had been mounted on the walls of the grotto in the early days. Perhaps they, too, could add their prayers of thanksgiving for the Virgin's intercession in the form of small plaques that line the interior of the original basilica to this day.

The faith of international pilgrims arriving in a constant stream to where healing waters were said to flow is what has allowed Lourdes and its heavenly messages for prayer, penance, and conversion to take root and flourish, despite secular efforts at the turn of the century to close the shrine down. This faith has been demonstrated not only in the afflicted, but those who journey with them as their aides and those who selflessly volunteer at the sanctuary to care for the incoming sick during their stay. None of this could have happened, however, if it weren't for the steadfast faith of a fourteen-year-old peasant girl named Bernadette, who was ready soil for what heaven had to till for her, France, and the world. It's time to hear the real story of Lourdes and meet the real Bernadette.

BERNADETTE: GROUNDED IN FAITH

In every sense of the word, Bernadette Soubirous was a woman of faith. The test of her faith began in the very earliest years of her life. Born to Catholic peasants, François and Louise Soubirous, on January 7, 1844, Bernadette's first test involved bouts with various illnesses. By the age of six, she had wrestled with stomach trouble, a spleen disorder, and chronic asthma, which made breathing difficult. By eleven, she had contracted cholera, which worsened her asthma and stunted her growth to a child-like stature of four-foot-eight.

As Bernadette struggled to recover from cholera, her parents struggled to make ends meet at the Boly flour mill, the first home to Bernadette and her three younger siblings. A depressed economy, recent drought, and the industrialization occurring in the larger cities of France all took their toll on the small family business in the mountainous town of Lourdes.

The family soon found themselves forced to close the mill and seek cramped quarters in the poorest section of town.

Bernadette was unable to attend formal school due to her illness, finances, and the need to help her family at home. Her lack of academic and religious education alienated her from children her own age and it was a great disappointment not to be able to receive her First Holy Communion with her peers.

By the time Bernadette turned thirteen, her family was evicted from the slum in which they had been living. François could not find work adequate to sustain his family. When the family was on the street with nowhere to turn, a relative took pity on them and offered the former one-room town jail, le Cachot, which was no longer considered fit, even for prisoners. The damp and musty hovel so aggravated Bernadette's asthma that her parents decided to send her to live with a family farther up in the Pyrenees in the town of Bartrès, where she would serve as nanny and shepherdess. It was hoped that the clean air, dry sleeping conditions, and ample food would improve the child's health and that she would have an opportunity to learn her catechism there. Besides, as François reasoned, it would mean one less mouth for him to feed.

Bartrès, however, presented its own difficulties. The woman of the household worked the young teen hard. While caring for the children, the house, and the sheep, she saw that there was no time to attend catechism class, the sole reason Bernadette had agreed to go to Bartrès in the first place. As a compromise, the woman attempted to teach Bernadette herself. This arrangement was most unpleasant because the Catechism was written in French and not the local dialect that Bernadette spoke. The young girl was simply unable to grasp it. The woman grew so impatient with her uneducated pupil that she finally threw the book across the room and shouted, "You'll never know anything!"

Bernadette learned quickly to be silent in the face of harsh treatment, a character trait that would serve her well in life. When questioned about it later by a cousin, she replied simply, "I thought God wanted this. When we think, God permits this, we don't complain." At the same time, however, Bernadette had made up her mind not to allow Bartrès to stand in the way of her receiving First Holy Communion; her heart was set on this sacrament. Four months later, just after her fourteenth birthday, Bernadette returned to Lourdes to finish her catechesis, despite the hardship and poverty that awaited her. Little did she know that the one who would truly prepare her for the sacraments would be none other than the Mother of God herself.

A Vision at Massabielle

Bernadette certainly had reason to grumble about her severe state of health and poverty that winter, but it was not her nature to complain. She was generally cheerful and content with life. Even then, her philosophy was, "When we wish for nothing, we always have what we need."

On the morning of February 11, 1858, Bernadette, in typical fashion, was pleading with her mother to be given permission to collect firewood with her sister and a friend. Louise didn't like the idea of her asthmatic child going out into the cold rain, but she knew how Bernadette detested feeling useless. Reluctantly she gave her consent, instructing her daughter to wear her stockings and a hood. That bleak winter day would forever change Bernadette, Lourdes, and the world.

The three girls hurried down the path, avoiding private property at all costs as they did not want to be accused of stealing. Soon they found themselves walking along a small canal until it joined with the Gave, a large river that ran through the town of Lourdes. At the place where the two bodies of water merged rose a thirty-foot rock wall called Massabielle, and to the girls' delight, they saw several sticks of wood washed up in the hollowed-out area at the base of the wall. Bernadette's sister and her friend tossed their shoes across the water and splashed across the canal. Bernadette, knowing her mother would be furious if she entered the icy water, asked the girls to carry her across, but they were cold and tired and anxious to get home.

Bernadette sat down on a rock and removed her shoes and stockings, still determined to help. As she did, she heard the sound of wind, although the trees across the river did not appear to be moving. Looking behind her toward the grotto, she noticed a wild rosebush growing in a niche high in the rock. Its branches were swaying frantically back and forth. As Bernadette stared at this strange display, she saw a bright light inside the niche, from which emerged a beautiful and illuminated young lady wearing a long white dress and veil, a blue sash around her waist, and a golden rose on each foot. Bernadette noticed the young lady had a large set of rosary beads hanging from her arm. Instinctively she attempted to reach in her pocket for her own beads, but she found herself frozen in fear, unable to move or speak. When the lady made the Sign of the Cross, Bernadette found she was able to do the same, and suddenly all fear left her. Kneeling, she began to pray the words of the Rosary, a prayer her family said together each night, while the dazzling young lady smiled and passed the beads through her fingers without moving her lips. Then in a flash, the vision disappeared.

When the girls returned with their bundles of wood, they noticed immediately that something was different about Bernadette. She seemed to have more strength and energy than usual and was asking them curious questions about whether they had seen anything or anyone. After some prodding by the girls, Bernadette shared her experience. She begged the girls not to tell, but her sister promptly told their mother, who punished Bernadette for making up such stories. She forbade Bernadette from going there again.

The Lady Speaks

Because of her obedient nature, Bernadette was immediately conflicted. She did not want to disobey her parents' orders to stay away from the grotto. On the other hand, she felt irresistibly drawn to return. She took the matter to a local priest in the form of her first Confession. He was intrigued by the girl's story of the wind and the vision and informed the pastor, Abbé Peyramale, who wanted no part of such nonsense.

Perhaps strengthened by the sacrament, Bernadette was eventually able to gain permission from her parents to make a second visit to Massabielle. François and Louise hoped this would cure Bernadette once and for all of her fantasies. Bernadette turned to the Church for protection and took a bottle of holy water with her to sprinkle on the apparition to test if it was from the devil. A group of schoolgirls excitedly accompanied Bernadette on this visit. When they arrived at the grotto, she fell to her knees and began to pray. As the girls watched in amazement, Bernadette's face grew ghostly pale and her eyes remained fixed on the niche above them. Even a large rock, tossed down the hill by some other schoolgirls as a prank, went completely unnoticed by the visionary. The frightened girls tried to wake their friend to no avail. Fearing her dead, they ran to get help from a nearby miller. He was a large and strapping man, yet it took all his strength to lift the small child and carry her to his home. By the time Louise arrived on the scene, Bernadette had regained her senses, only to have them nearly knocked out of her by her angry mother.

It took the strong persuasion of a wealthy townswoman, a former customer of Louise, to convince Bernadette's mother to allow her daughter to visit the grotto for a third time. The woman accompanied Bernadette and brought with her a pen and paper to acquire the name of the illuminated visitor. When the visitor appeared, Bernadette prayed the Rosary as usual. At the conclusion of the prayer, she took a step closer to the apparition and held out the pen and paper. The lady glided down through the back of the niche into the hollow of the rock below and came quite close to Bernadette. She began to speak in a most serene and lovely voice. She smiled at the sight of the pen and paper and said it was not necessary. Instead she asked, "Would you have the kindness to come here for fifteen days?" Bernadette was delighted to be conversing with the lady and happily agreed. Just being in the lady's presence filled her with indescribable joy, and she could think of nothing more than to see her again. Ominously the illuminated visitor would also tell Bernadette, "I cannot promise to make you happy in this life, but in the next."

Crowds and Controversy

It didn't take long for word about the visions to spread throughout Lourdes and the surrounding area, which put sudden and intense attention on the impoverished fourteen-year-old and her family. People were quite divided over the matter. Many scoffed at the child and called her a clown and a liar, which Bernadette bore with patience and silence. In reality, she was more scandalized by those who clamored to touch her or snip a lock of her hair in misguided adoration. Some claimed this was all a trick of the devil, while others believed the vision in the grotto was actually an answer to their prayers: the Virgin Mary had come to save their country! At the time, France was going through a period of rapid secularization. The once-religious nation was now closing churches and throwing clergy into prison in some of the larger cities. Anything that smacked of superstition was considered downright dangerous. For Bernadette, none of the personal opinions or politics concerned her. All that mattered to her was keeping her promise to the beautiful lady in the grotto.

As the crowds grew, so did the controversy. The police were anxious to put an end to the matter and summoned Bernadette for interrogation. They threatened her with jail, but she was surprisingly calm and unafraid. The police commissioner twisted her words to try and confuse her, but she corrected his errors and repeated without exaggeration or embellishment what she had been seeing and hearing in the grotto. She could not promise the police that she would stay away from Massabielle, for she had already given her word to the lady that she would return. This was a promise she intended to keep.

By the eighth apparition, Bernadette began to exhibit rather strange behavior. Her mood became much more somber. Hundreds watched as she crawled on her knees in the filth of the grotto floor, where herds of pigs had often been brought for watering. She even kissed the dirty ground reverently. During the ninth apparition, the visionary began digging in the far corner of the grotto. To the disgust of onlookers, she drank muddy water, washed her face in it, and even ate some wild grass growing nearby. Many thought Bernadette had gone mad. Later she explained that the lady had asked her to do these unpleasant things as a penance for sins, both hers and others. Performing acts of penance for sin would become an important mission that Bernadette would carry out for the rest of her life. As a confirmation for her faithfulness to the lady, a spring of water soon bubbled forth from the place where Bernadette had been digging, and within twenty-four hours miracles began to be reported as a result of that water.

Request for a Procession and Chapel

In the twelfth apparition, the lady told Bernadette that she wanted a chapel to be erected at the grotto and for priests and people to come in procession. Bernadette obediently went to Abbé Peyramale to deliver this message. The pastor of Lourdes was well aware of the so-called visions at Massabielle. He was also aware of the marked increase in the numbers of people showing up for Mass and Confession. Still, he dismissed the matter as utter nonsense and did not appreciate that it was happening in his parish. When Bernadette appeared at his rectory door, the pastor was surprised at her tiny size and quiet demeanor. He demanded to know what she wanted. At the mention of a procession, Abbé Peyramale lost his temper and chased the girl away. It wasn't until she was halfway home that Bernadette realized she had not told him about the chapel. She bravely returned that evening to the rectory, but the request for a chapel made his impatience flair again. He would not discuss the matter further until this vision identified herself.

When Bernadette reported the pastor's response to the illuminated lady in next apparition, she only smiled and made her request again. So the visionary paid a second visit to the rectory. Abbé Peyramale was not going to comply with such stubbornness. This time he demanded not only the name of the lady, but a sign: that the rosebush growing in the niche in the grotto bloom even though it was still winter. Otherwise, there would be no more talk of a procession or chapel.

At the fifteenth apparition, an unprecedented audience of ten thousand squeezed into the grotto area and the fields beyond. People had traveled from as far as Paris for the big day, when surely the heavenly visitor would identify herself and perform a great miracle. Contrary to their expectations, nothing seemed to happen. Bernadette arrived, received her apparition, and left quietly. There was no proclamation and no miracle. The crowds left disappointed, but Bernadette was content. No, she had not acquired the lady's name, but she had delivered her message faithfully to the pastor and she had kept her promise of coming to the grotto fifteen times. Bernadette considered the event over.

Three weeks later, however, on the Feast of the Annunciation, Bernadette woke from her sleep with that familiar urging to hurry to the grotto. Obediently, she slipped out of bed into the early dawn to greet the lady. This time, Bernadette was insistent on getting the visitor's name and asked her repeatedly. At the fourth request, the lady stopped smiling, raised her eyes to heaven and answered solemnly, "I am the Immaculate Conception." These words were strange to Bernadette, and logically so, for this was brand new theology promulgated by the Church only four years earlier, and it was highly unlikely that an uneducated peasant like Bernadette would have heard or understood this title for the Mother of God. Anxious to tell Abbé Peyramale, she repeated the words to herself over and over until she reached the rectory and announced them triumphantly to an astonished pastor. For him, the events at Massabielle suddenly took on a whole new meaning.

Bernadette in the Limelight

When the news broke that the vision at Lourdes claimed to be the Virgin Mary, crowds swarmed the grotto to build altars where they could leave gifts of flowers and money.

The police tried to barricade the area, but fences were torn down by the faithful as soon as they had been erected. In the meanwhile, to her great joy and after much anticipation, Bernadette received her First Holy Communion. She saw the Virgin two more times before the apparitions came to an end. Bernadette expected life to return to normal, but the mania surrounding the visionary and her family was only beginning. People barged into the Soubirous abode at all hours, demanding to see Bernadette, wanting her to bless their holy objects, or pray over a sick loved one. "I have no power!" Bernadette protested. "I am not a priest!"

Constant offerings of food and money were made to the struggling family, but Bernadette was adamant about not accepting any of it. If someone tried to sneak coins into her pocket, she claimed they were burning her and would throw them immediately across the room. She wished to remain poor and made that point very clear. It was apparent that Bernadette had learned many things from the Virgin, including an appreciation for her state of poverty, littleness, and ignorance. It was why, she testified, the Virgin had appeared to her in the first place. "If the Blessed Virgin chose me, it's because I am the most ignorant. If she had found a girl more ignorant than I, that's the one she would have chosen."

Bernadette also understood that her role was not just to be a mouthpiece for heaven's directives. She had to live the messages of prayer, penance, and conversion in order to be "happy not in this world, but in the next." She had to be an example of holy living. Despite what people thought, the visionary was no more guaranteed heaven than anyone else. Bernadette would have to earn her heaven by overcoming pride, accepting suffering, and serving others. She knew that wealth and vanity were not going to help her achieve that goal.

Immediately following the final apparition in July 1858, the bishop of Tarbes initiated a formal investigation. When questioned, Bernadette demonstrated common sense and openness. She was neither shy nor boastful. She spoke only when spoken to with answers that were short, to the point, and exceedingly consistent. The teen did not seek attention or claim to be a wonder worker; in fact, she rejected such claims. Her humility and sincerity were impeccable and this would play a major part of the bishop's decision to eventually approve the apparitions. As he would later attest, the best proof of the authenticity of the apparitions was Bernadette herself.

Life at the Hospice

With a formal Church investigation underway, Abbé Peyramale made it his charge to protect Bernadette's humility at all costs. He knew if the visions were authenticated, Bernadette could be a candidate for eventual sainthood; and he was unwilling to allow any chance of her falling into scandal. The priest frequently admonished the child in public and discouraged any kind of adoration of her to guard her humility. He saw to it that François had work opportunities to enable the family to move into modest but more appropriate housing, but something had to be done about the growing crowds. Two years after the apparitions, he decided to have Bernadette board with the Sisters of Charity from Nevers who ran a hospice, school, and boarding home at Lourdes. Here the visionary would be protected from the prying eye of the public while the investigations of the apparitions were being conducted.

It was not easy for Bernadette to move out of her home, but she adapted quickly to her new surroundings. She had already been dreaming of living a hidden and religious life, perhaps with the Carmelites; but her poor health would not permit her to follow their strict rule. In the meantime, the Sisters of Charity taught Bernadette how to read and write, sew and embroider. It was while helping in the hospice that Bernadette discovered she had a calling to serve the sick and dying and a gift for working with the youngest children in the school.

Aside from her association with the events in the grotto, Bernadette was a normal youngster. She was gentle, simple, patient, and friendly with the sisters. She joked and laughed at recreation. She helped as her health allowed; and even when having violent asthma attacks, she never complained. Although living and working at the hospice helped remove her from the general public, there was no end to the visitors who were given special permission to meet Bernadette and listen to her story. This was a great trial for the girl because she was already working on becoming little and hidden, but she complied with great patience and charity. Abbé Peyramale had carefully instructed the sisters to protect Bernadette's humility, so they followed his lead by telling visitors that she was worth nothing. That was just fine with Bernadette, who readily agreed.

Formal approval of the apparitions came in 1862, just four years after the event at Massabielle. This attracted even more visitors to the hospice, interrupting Bernadette's work, solitude, and recreation. Many religious orders invited her to join their communities, but she did not feel called to any of them. Her decision in the end was to join the Sisters of Charity with whom she lived. To become a professed sister, however, presented Bernadette with one of her greatest trials of all: to leave her family, hometown, and beloved grotto and relocate hundreds of miles away to the motherhouse in the city of Nevers. "Lourdes is not heaven," she said, accepting that her work in Lourdes was over. Her precious grotto, like Bernadette herself, was already undergoing severe changes.

The rugged terrain was being tamed to accommodate hundreds of thousands of visitors from all over Europe. In answer to the Virgin's request for a chapel, a large underground crypt church had been built directly above the grotto, the first of several basilicas that would be erected on and near the site of the apparitions.

The Motherhouse at Nevers

In July 1866, Bernadette formally entered the motherhouse at Nevers to begin her religious life. The superiors were fully aware of the difficult task that was before them. They could not afford to treat Bernadette with any special favor, as she was now an authentic visionary and could potentially be scrutinized for sainthood one day. Therefore, they took extra measures in addition to the strict rule of the day to humble Bernadette at every juncture. They had her dress in her peasant clothing and tell her story only once to the entire community; then she was forbidden to discuss the matter again.

This arrangement suited Bernadette. She was eager to be left alone to work on her spiritual perfection but in a way that was most secretive and hidden from her superiors. Fortunately for us, the young visionary recorded some of her poignant moments of resolve and discovery on the pages of a notebook during her thirteen years as a religious. These insights, translated into a book titled *A Holy Life: The Writings of St. Bernadette of Lourdes*, would give important clues to the spirituality behind this saint-in-progress, for that's what she truly was. As Bernadette wrote in her notebook, she had to become a "great saint" because of the graces she had been given. This would not entail great works, but small and deliberate ways of mastering her self-will and uniting it to the will of God. It took persistent acts of self-denial and submission, day after day, to walk the spiritual journey she had laid out for herself. All of this went largely unnoticed by her community; to the others, Bernadette did not seem excessively pious or extraordinary. She was obedient to the rules of the order (particularly silence), cheerful and charitable toward others, unpretentious, easily accepting of correction, and willing to take on the lowliest duties. The depth of her holiness would only be appreciated after her death and as revealed through the pages of her journal.

A little over a year after her admittance to Nevers, Bernadette and her fellow novices professed their vows in a ceremony with the bishop that culminated with an assignment at one of the religious houses in France. Bernadette was the only one in her class not to receive an assignment. The superiors and the bishop claimed she was good for nothing, and therefore she would remain at the motherhouse. They crafted this plan purposefully, knowing that the motherhouse would provide better protection for Bernadette than the other houses, but they could not let the newly professed sister know that.

Unfortunately, the motherhouse at Nevers was not much better than the hospice at Lourdes at sheltering Bernadette from visitors. There was always a bishop, a dignitary, or a historian who had been granted special permission to meet with Bernadette in the parlor to listen to her story. She was even required to pose for a photography session in peasant clothing, which she found most distasteful. Still, the visionary wiped her tears when being summoned and greeted each visitor with charity and patience.

Trials continued to be a part of Bernadette's journey, but the young sister understood that trials served to detach people from their desires, so she learned to embrace them instead of fearing or rejecting them. In addition to the trial of constant visitors that disrupted her work and prayer, the family that Bernadette had left behind in Lourdes was also a source of frequent grief and hardship for the exiled nun. She lost both of her parents which caused her great pain and sorrow. There were also family squabbles, which she attempted to resolve through letters. Bernadette mourned for her sister, who suffered repeated miscarriages, and corrected her younger brothers, who needed constant guidance. She was deeply disappointed to learn that some of her family members were becoming wealthy by selling souvenirs at the grotto, and she worried for their salvation.

There was another terrifying suffering for Bernadette as years began to separate her from the events that had taken place at Massabielle. For the first time, she was beginning to forget the details. Her mind became more and more confused, and this caused her great agony. She had taken such care to report every detail truthfully all her life, but now dates, times, and names were slipping from her memory. Even the Lady of Light seemed to be growing dimmer in her mind. Bernadette agonized at the thought of remembering something incorrectly, and insisted that people refer to her original testimonies that had been recorded by the Church. Her deepest mental anguish was the realization of how tremendously she had been graced and the fear that she had not lived up to that grace. This was not something she wrote about extensively in her journal, but cryptic comments to others revealed the dark night she seemed to be experiencing in later years. "It's really painful not to be able to breathe (referring to her asthma), but it's much more agonizing to be tortured by spiritual distress. It's terrifying."

Her Last "Assignment"

Winters made Bernadette's asthma severe, and it was not uncommon for her to be placed in the infirmary to recuperate. At times, her breathing was so labored that she became weakened to the point at which a priest was summoned to give her the Anointing of the Sick. She was patient with her illness, saying, "The Good Lord sends it. I must accept it." When

Bernadette wasn't a patient in the infirmary, she worked there, mixing remedies, changing bandages, and encouraging the sick. She was an excellent nurse whose empathy was likely based in her own experience of physical suffering. She knew how to listen to patients and give them sound physical and spiritual advice, which relaxed and reassured them. For Bernadette, no task was too repulsive when it came to the sick and dying. "When you nurse a patient, you must withdraw before giving thanks," she would explain to the younger sisters. "We are sufficiently rewarded by the honor of being attentive to her."

In the last five years of Bernadette's life, she contracted tuberculosis of the lung and bone. She had to confine herself to bed in the infirmary, knowing that this time she would not recover. She had to submit to the sisters to do everything for her and was unable to follow the rules of the order. It was a great trial for Bernadette to be truly "good for nothing." Still she was courageous and creative in her suffering. She called her infirmary bed with the tent-like piece of linen suspended above it her "white chapel." It was here that she would begin what she called her "last assignment"—prayer and sacrifice—for she was unable to offer anything else. She made a pact with the Lord to offer her suffering each day for the conversion of one sinner, the identity of whom only the Lord and Blessed Virgin would know.

As a painful tumor on her knee, bed sores, stomach ailments, chest pains, and slow suffocation grew in intensity, Bernadette removed the holy cards and pictures she had pinned to her bed curtains and kept only her crucifix in her hands at all times. She offered herself as a victim for the heart of Jesus and needed nothing but him. "I'm happier with my crucifix on my bed of pain than a queen on her throne," she declared in earnest. She did her best to suffer in silence as not to disturb the other patients and talked of heaven and how she would take prayer with her there, where it would be more powerful. In her final days, Bernadette seemed fully united with the passion of Christ. She had achieved a total emptying of self. Struggling for her last breaths and perhaps reflective of her childhood at the Boly flour mill, she said, "I'm being ground down like a grain of wheat."

Bernadette Soubirous passed away on April 16, 1879, at the age of thirty-five. So many mourners came to pay their respects that her little body was displayed for several days in the chapel. The cause for her canonization was opened twenty-eight years after her death. When her body was exhumed for the investigation, it was found to be perfectly incorrupt. She was beatified on June 14, 1926, and canonized—appropriately—on December 8, 1933, the Feast of the Immaculate Conception. Bernadette's sainthood was granted, not because she had been privileged to see the Virgin Mary, but because of the heroic virtue she displayed throughout her life. Pope Pius XI declared the saint's virtues publicly:

> There is no doubt that here we are in the presence of saintliness in the exact and precise sense of the word. Indeed, when we consider the life of Bernadette . . . it can be summed up in three words: Bernadette was faithful to her mission, she was humble in her glory, and she was strong when she was put to the test. (Pope Pius XI, *"Decree on the heroic nature of the virtues of the Venerable Sister Marie-Bernard Soubirous"*)

Today the body of St. Bernadette Soubirous remains on display in a gold-and-glass casket at the motherhouse in Nevers. Millions have come to reverence her incorrupt body and pray before it. Considering how in life Bernadette abhorred being stared at as some kind of anomaly and would respond to this by withdrawing into the hood of her peasant clothing and later into the veil of her habit, one might wonder if this was not a final act of self-sacrifice with which to glorify God. For surely if God had asked such a favor of Bernadette, she would have given him the only answer she had ever given him and Blessed Mother—yes!

Faithful to the End

Bernadette Soubirous had her faith tested from the start. Her dire poverty and serious health issues could have left her bitter, but she never complained or questioned God about the justness of it all. She had a simple but firm belief in her Catholic faith that she had inherited from her parents, who likewise showed gratitude to God despite their great difficulties. Holy Mass and family Rosary were important to her. Receiving the Holy Communion and the Sacrament of Penance were top priorities that would become staples in her religious life. Imitating the example of her parents, Louise and François, Bernadette was generous and hospitable to others with a particular affection for the sick and poor.

It is fair to say that Bernadette was already living the message of Lourdes—prayer, penance, and conversion—long before the apparitions began. She was being graced and prepared in a special way through her life of poverty and illness, and the apparitions would call the world's attention to that. As much as the apparitions were about the Virgin Mary and heaven, they were also about the example of Bernadette and how she responded to it all.

Bernadette believed in the scriptures that said the poor are blessed. She recognized that God kept things from the learned that he wished to reveal to the little ones. She considered herself blessed to be counted among those little ones and had no attraction to wealth or fame. In France in the mid-1800s, poverty was derided and middle-class capitalism, fueled by industrial revolution, frequently exploited people— even children—to achieve its selfish ends. Yet Bernadette could not be corrupted by the mentality of the world. She was and always would be free from attachment to material things and free to not worry about the future; instead, she lived day-to-day, relying on him who was the source of life.

From the beginning, Bernadette had complete confidence and trust in the lady in the grotto. No person or situation could shake the faith that Bernadette held in the apparitions she received—not even the threat of imprisonment. Her fidelity to her promise and her mission was unquestionable. It was this unswerving faith that convinced many critics of Lourdes to eventually accept her story as truth. Bernadette's faithful deliverance and living of the messages were as undeniable, as the healing powers of the water she helped to bring forth through yet another act of faith. It was only natural that she would be attracted to a religious order that was founded on the exact same principles as the messages of Lourdes: prayer, penance, poverty, service of souls, and charity to the sick and poor. It was a living gospel, a perfect complement to the words of the Virgin.

Bernadette's faith, as firm as the rock of Massabielle, would deepen the faith of millions. Pilgrims from all walks of life have come and continue to come to kneel at the location where she had once knelt, to gaze up at the same niche in the grotto, and to ask the same Virgin's intercession for themselves or loved ones. Countless lives have been touched physically, spiritually, and emotionally, making Lourdes one of the largest healing centers in the world for people of all faiths and one of the most visited Marian shrines in history.

Like Faustina and Thérèse who would come after her, Bernadette was a woman of heroic virtue, especially when it came to faith. She held fast to her goal of heaven and, according to the Church, has attained that goal. Unlike Faustina and Thérèse, however, she did not leave us with great spiritual writings, save for some brief reflections in her notebook.

Bernadette instead taught by example. She modeled the faith we are all called to have, and miraculous things happened as a result. They are still happening. What wondrous things might we unleash if we were to follow this saint's powerful example?

Lessons in Faith
from Bernadette

M y pilgrimage to Lourdes turned out to be a journey of
discovery. I came to know not only the real Bernadette
and the meaning of the apparitions, but I learned about
myself in the process as well. In speaking with the experts of
the sanctuary, I grew in understanding that Lourdes is not a
quaint tourist destination or a historical museum. It is a living
sanctuary with as much relevance today as it had a century
and a half ago, because Lourdes is the message of the Gospel
and therefore is a path to happiness. For so many people lost
in a world of darkness, unsure of their bearings, Lourdes is a
beacon of light. It helps people find their way and gives them
strength for the journey. Lourdes provides an invitation for
true conversion by allowing pilgrims to encounter Christ
through sacraments and prayer, to make acts of penance, and

to turn their hearts and lives over to God. It is an opportunity to discover, define, and deepen their faith.

During my time in Lourdes, I had a chance to reflect on the appearance of the Virgin in a less-than-immaculate grotto to a child of lowly status and compromised health. I saw in this a great message for all people. While the apparitions are over, the message most certainly is not. God chose this unique encounter to speak powerfully through Mary to meet not just Bernadette, but all of us where we are in life, in the midst of our poverty and failures. He comes to tell us that he loves us just as we are, with our successes but also with our wounds, our weaknesses, and our limitations. He offers forgiveness for our sinfulness and invites us to turn from the world and its materialism and embrace instead a deep and meaningful spiritual life. This is wonderful and freeing news. God also asks of us something important, and that is to in turn love and serve our fellow humanity in their physical and spiritual poverty. We are called to increase our faithfulness and live a life dedicated to loving and serving God and his people, seeing him especially in the poor, sick, and marginalized. Lourdes, therefore, is a call to action.

A Sense of Compassion

As I got to know Bernadette, especially through the pages of her journal, I found I liked her instantly. I did not see her as a plastic figure kneeling in prayer with her hands folded at all times. There was genuineness and boldness about her that reminded me of Jo from Little Women, one of my favorite childhood literary heroines. Bernadette was of the earth, loving nature and preferring to be in the mountainous outdoors as a youngster; and she was down-to-earth as well, a trait she would never outgrow. There was nothing prissy or pretentious about this young girl; she simply told it like it was. While she certainly took her mission seriously, Bernadette enjoyed life and looked for opportunities to introduce levity. She had a delightful sense of humor that she judiciously revealed to her family or the sisters in her community in an effort to lift their spirits. She was a true friend to those around her. I was struck at how life-giving Bernadette was in her interactions. Whether it was for the nosey visitors clamoring to see her or for the sick and dying, whom she tenderly cared for in the infirmary, Bernadette acted on their behalf and not her own. She was a giver, sustained by her love for God and the Blessed Mother, and that challenged me to give more generously of myself in my own circles of influence.

Bernadette helped me to be more compassionate in my giving as well. After my pilgrimage to Lourdes, I found a greater appreciation for the sick and suffering. I became more active in cooking meals for those in need, taking the Eucharist to shut-ins, and providing emotional support to those facing advanced age and death. Over the years, my husband and I have shared our Lourdes water (brought home from our pilgrimage) with numerous individuals, prayed with them, and even helped to send two different friends to the sanctuary for their special healing needs. Bernadette showed me the joy in serving others when done in a spirit of love.

Faith in Mary

Another important way Bernadette impacted my spirituality was that she awakened in me a desire to have a relationship with the Blessed Virgin like hers. Perhaps it was the simplicity of the mother-daughter love I saw between the two of them that was so attractive to me. The Queen of Heaven came as a beckoning, welcoming, smiling mother who wanted to be near her children on earth to impart words of encouragement and wrap them in her mantle of protection. Bernadette responded with total love and openness to the Virgin and was devoted to her for the remainder of her life. She was not intimidated by the Virgin's perfection or holiness; rather, she sought to please her in everything she did and said.

I enjoyed being allowed a peek into this special bond between the heavenly Mother and earthly daughter, because I myself had never had a relationship with the Blessed Mother in my youth. Mary was a strictly Catholic phenomenon. I don't recall ever talking about her in Sunday school, and the only depiction we had of her at home was as a small figure in a manger set that we displayed during the Christmas season. It was certainly not a holy relic; my sisters and I played with that wooden stable like it was a dollhouse until most of the figurines ended up with cracks and missing body parts. After the holidays, Mary and her friends were packed in the basement with the rest of the Christmas cornucopia.

It is all the more ironic, therefore, that the day in my childhood when I heard God whisper in my eight-year-old heart that he had a special mission for me, I immediately thought it had something to do with the Virgin Mary. Embarrassed as I am to admit this, I even thought for a while after that experience that I was to be another Virgin Mary, although that didn't seem to have any sound biblical basis. I just remember the feeling of secretly being chosen for something and that maybe it had to do with Mary herself. I cannot tell you why this thought would have ever entered my head at the time.

It would actually take thirty-seven years to get an answer to this mystery. At that point, I had just attended a women's retreat in which the leaders had taken us back in our memories to our earliest recollections of God. I spent a great deal of time that weekend meditating on my "conversation" with God at eight years old. Although it wasn't necessarily my earliest experience of him, it was certainly a poignant one. During that retreat, I felt immensely blessed and quite undeserving that God would have taken the trouble to come to me, a nominally churched kid, and let me know he had a plan for my life. It truly gave me great hope and inspiration to figure out exactly what that mission might be. Since I had become an adult, I was pretty confident that I had grown into my mission as a wife, mother, and Catholic author and speaker.

Two days after the retreat, I was sitting in the back of church for daily Mass with our youngest on my lap. Something the priest said in his homily made me recount that special childhood experience. I couldn't help but smile sheepishly at the thought of how precocious I had been to ask the King and Creator of the universe if I might actually become another Blessed Mother. At once, I heard the voice again. "No, you are going to glorify my Mother." The words were so unexpected, powerful, and intimate that I immediately began to weep. I kept repeating the words in my head . . . "You are going to glorify my Mother, glorify my Mother." I could not have possibly heard correctly. Why me? I had not been raised in a Catholic family. I didn't grow up praying the family Rosary. I never went to parochial school or crowned the statue of the Virgin on May crowning. How could I, a former Protestant and still feeling a bit like an adopted child, glorify the Mother?

My relationship with the Virgin was, at best, a work in progress. Granted, some of the saints had helped pave the way for me, particularly St. Louis de Montfort and his True Devotion to Mary. I recognized the Virgin's value as the greatest of all saints, a fierce advocate against Satan, and a model of holiness for Christian disciples and particularly for women as wives and mothers. Maybe that was my hang-up: while Mary was magnifying the Lord, her perfect virtue seemed to magnify only my lack of perfection. My pilgrimage to Medjugorje seemed to have improved things somewhat. There she became more accessible to me, especially as I observed the deep, personal relationship so many pilgrims had with her, fondly calling her "Mama Mary" and other endearing terms. Still, my personal relationship with the Blessed Mother at that point in my life was based more on sincere respect and admiration than close intimate friendship.

Bernadette helped change that for me. She helped me to see that Mary truly is the mother of us all, a loving mother who has come to guide and protect her children. Having lost my earthly mother when I was twenty-eight, I had forgotten how important the mother role is in our lives, no matter how old we are. We all need a mom . . . and what a mom she is! She is relentless in her love and protection, and is full of grace and wisdom. It was Bernadette who instilled in my heart a desire to work for the Blessed Mother's intentions with total joy and commitment. Professionally, I've written books on the Virgin and have spoken on her as well, but I would hardly consider my mission of glorifying her to be fulfilled. I'm sure that will be a lifelong process.

Financial Crisis

One of the lessons Bernadette learned and internalized from the Virgin in the grotto was that material poverty—even the extreme form that she and her family faced—was nothing compared to spiritual poverty, a disease that the world suffered from then and increasingly suffers from today. Her total trust and reliance on Our Lord and Our Lady for everything she needed helped me immensely to persevere through a recent family financial crisis of my own. It began almost five years ago, when my husband woke from his sleep in a sweaty panic. A deep and troubling reality had hit him full force: after twenty years, he had lost his lucrative consulting business. It was a way of life that had afforded us the ability to raise our four boys in a comfortable and stable environment with enough flexibility for me to stay home and for Mark to spend more time with his kids than most dads. For a long time we had talked about the possibility of his job ending. Worrisome signs began to appear on the horizon and the economy continued to falter, but the cold, hard fact of unemployment was now at our doorstep. Fortunately, we had been good savers all our married life, and had money to live on. But as time wore on and no solid leads were in sight for full-time employment, we grew more and more concerned.

Each month we watched our savings accounts drain, and there was little money coming in to stem the tide. It felt like we were in a room with all four walls closing in on us and there was no escape hatch. We went through the motions of life, taking turns having emotional meltdowns. I think we must have gone through all the painful steps of grieving our loss—shock, denial, guilt, anger, bargaining, and depression. I was desperate to figure out how this could have happened and what we could do to prevent it from ever happening again. I wanted to know from God why it had happened. Weren't we good and faithful followers, always going out of our way to serve others and do the right thing? Why would God punish us like this? Would we lose the house and be on the street with four mouths to feed? What about the ministries God had entrusted to us? Was it all for naught? I remember one night crying in bed like a little child, with loud, pitiful moans and sobs. Resurfacing in me were panicky memories from my childhood when my father's telephone company would go on strike for long periods of time and we were at risk of losing everything. Where was God in all of this, and why wasn't he coming to our rescue?

It felt as though my head were in a vice, being squeezed tighter with each passing day. Some days it became difficult to breathe or just get out of bed. Our mantra, week after excruciating week, was Faustina's words: "Jesus, I trust in you." We said this prayer over and over and over. Looking back now, I realize that when I was initially praying to be trusting, it was always with an outcome attached. Jesus I trust in you . . . to work this all out. Jesus . . . restore our losses. Jesus . . . return us to financial security. Please make us better off than were before. It seemed that every time my husband sat down and cracked open the Bible for inspiration, it fell open to the story of Job, which only further exacerbated the situation. Mark had no desire to be Job. He did not intend to lose everything and everyone around him, and he told God so, rather adamantly. Nothing changed and our future looked no brighter.

At particularly low times, I would threaten God that if he didn't fix things, I would. I told him I would walk away from my writing/speaking ministry and return to the work world full-time. I searched job listings on the Internet and I interviewed without success. God was not opening any doors for us. He seemed to want us to remain just where we were. Eventually, Mark and I began to cease in our struggle and become more docile about our situation. I think it had more to do with sheer exhaustion than sheer faith.

One day, I decided to read Job. I needed to remind myself how it all turned out for this just man who had been sorely tried at every level. I read how one-by-one, Job's friends came to visit him and offer him explanations of why so many bad things had happened to him. There had to be a reason, they argued. Job rejected all of their ideas. Finally, toward the end of the chapter, God himself speaks. He doesn't, however, give Job a reason for the chain of events. He doesn't need to explain himself, for he is God. He points out that Job's friends were wrong in their surmising and, in fact, Job was right not to question God or his motives. Because of Job's faithfulness, God restores his losses, even with added abundance. This patient faithfulness in the midst of suffering reminded me suddenly of Bernadette. She never questioned why she was born less healthy than her friends and classmates, nor did she question why her family was the poorest in all of Lourdes. She accepted each hardship and each divine responsibility with a cheerful and willing heart for God to use fully.

Bernadette's unfailing faithfulness no matter the circumstances gave me the impetus to move from my "stuck" position. It wasn't enough to just say I trusted God anymore; it was time to begin putting my hope into action, and that required faith. I stopped trying to guess the reasons for our financial situation, what lessons we were supposed to learn, and when this ordeal would be over. In short, I stopped trying to be in control. I spent more time and energy handling the tasks that came my way and running the household as smoothly and normally as I could, and less time worrying about how we were going to pay the next bills. I tried my best to let God be God. It's not that I didn't have occasional relapses into fear and anxiety and frustration—I did—but I was learning to let go in faith—true faith.

Years later, we are still nowhere near where we once were financially. We are still climbing out of the hole and a great deal of uncertainty remains. We have come to accept the job loss and the fact that God has been very quiet during the last few years. His consolations, once plentiful, have been few and far between. But with this dark night of sorts has also come great growth in faith and virtue for my husband and me. The financial crisis has helped us to put things into perspective. We realize that our cross, as difficult as it is, is not nearly as large as the cross of others, and we are appreciative of that. On a practical level, we have learned to separate wants from needs. We are less impatient with one another and more grateful for what we have. We don't sweat the small stuff nearly as much and our bond as a family is stronger. I would say our marriage is in the best place it has ever been as we continue to turn things over to God.

An important lesson for me in this situation has been one of humility. All our married life we were privileged to be in a position of giving and we responded to that by trying to help those in need whenever we could. Now the tables are turned. We have had to learn to be on the receiving end of the generosity of others. It still isn't easy for me to accept the tithes of others, but I try and follow Bernadette's example of humble obedience and allow God to do as he wishes, knowing it is a gift for others to give, as we once were freer to do. Perhaps most significantly, this financial struggle has helped us to understand the meaning of "give us this day our daily bread." In a poignant way, our family has been forced to let go of the future and live in the present where God, who is faithful, gives us what we need. The proof is all around us: there is a roof over our heads, food on the table, and love in our hearts. I thank my spiritual journey partner Bernadette for helping us weather this challenging storm.

A Living Faith

In my thirty years of being a Catholic, three popes have held office: John Paul II, Benedict XVI, and Francis I. In a way, I look at these leaders as a holy trilogy, each building upon their predacessor. All three of these great shepherds have made it a focus during their papacies to inspire and encourage the Catholic faithful to have a living faith. A living faith requires an understanding of the tenets of that faith. It calls us to embrace that faith by applying it to our daily lives and putting those teachings into action. It invites us to share that faith which we have unpacked with enthusiasm with those we are blessed to meet.

When I consider Bernadette and her heroic virtue of faith, I think she would have made a perfect patron saint or poster child for the Year of Faith, recently celebrated in the Church on the fiftieth anniversary of the opening of the

Second Vatican Council. Pope Emeritus Benedict XVI, who recognized the vast spiritual poverty throughout the world—particularly in Western nations, because people no longer understood the richness of their Catholic faith—instituted this Year of Faith. It was an invitation for Catholics worldwide to re-experience their faith and make it their own. (This does not mean custom tailoring what we will believe to fit our personal lifestyle, but developing a vibrant and relevant faith to which we are wholly accountable.)

The three popes have invited us to open wide the door of faith and walk through it to rediscover the basics of Catholic identity, including the devotions, community celebrations, and the shared love for the Eucharist. They urge us to study the Apostles' Creed, the catechism, holy scripture, and the documents of Vatican II. Strengthened by a more regular participation in the Mass and the Sacrament of Reconciliation, we will be better able to take our faith to others and witness to the Gospel. In an increasingly secular culture where people seem unable to agree on fundamental right and wrong and where it is easy for people to undermine virtue, character, and moral judgment, faithful Catholics are called to be credible witnesses as people who love the Lord and entrust their lives to him. We are to become a living sign of the presence of the risen Lord in our otherwise darkened world.

I have seen through my work as a writer and speaker, and, more importantly, in my role as wife and mother, that having an enlivened Catholic faith is transforming for us and those around us. An enlivened faith is a contagious faith, but I've also come to recognize that it is contingent upon two things. First, to fully live the faith, we must know that faith. That means having a good working knowledge of what our Church teaches and why, and that takes study and prayer. Second, and equally important, our faith must be rooted in a personal relationship with Jesus Christ. It is not enough to know about Jesus; we must know him, because we cannot give Jesus to others if we do not have him ourselves. This personal relationship with our Lord needs to mature to the point where he becomes a real and living force so powerful in our lives that it alters the very way we think and act. As Saint Paul says, "It is no longer I who live, but Christ who lives in me" (Gal 2:20).

In a striking way, the efforts of our recent popes to engage Catholics in their faith echo the message of Lourdes that Bernadette received from heaven and that has endured for more than 150 years. It is a call for an authentic and renewed conversion through encountering Christ, intensifying our witness of charity to others, and reflecting on the nature of sin at work in our lives. If we respond to this call by committing to live our faith with zeal and conviction, as Bernadette exemplified so beautifully with her life, God can use that to affect the rest of the world in a real and positive way.

EPILOGUE

So where do we go from here on our spiritual journey? That is something for you and God to work out together through prayer, study, and a sacramental life. Perhaps there has been something mentioned in these chapters—a scriptural passage, a devotion, a papal writing, a Church teaching, or a saint's autobiography—that has inspired you to want to learn more. Or maybe something I've shared in my own struggles has given you new insight on a situation you are currently facing. Great! Then the book has more than served its purpose.

At the end of this book I've included two appendices for you. Appendix 1 contains three sets of reflection questions, one for each of the three saints who have been my spiritual companions. Perhaps these questions will guide and deepen your prayer, help you in leading a small-group conversation, or be starting points for contemplation. I've found that journaling often helps me uncover things God wants me to consider further. Perhaps these questions can assist your journaling. May they yield abundant spiritual fruit for your journey in whatever ways you choose to use them. Appendix 2 contains prayers that are mentioned in the book: "The Act of Oblation to Merciful Love" and "The Chaplet of Divine Mercy". The Act of Oblation to Merciful Love was created by St. Thérèse, wherein she would offer herself as a victim of love. The Chaplet of Divine Mercy was taught to Faustina by Jesus, to unite the pray-er with the sacrifice of Jesus. May these also strengthen you in your spiritual life and bring you closer to Christ.

Appendix One:
Reflection Questions

Reflection Questions: **Thérèse** *(Love)*

1. How and where am I most able to demonstrate my love for others?
2. What is there in me that hinders my ability to love freely and fruitfully?
3. In her community, Thérèse reached out to sisters whom no one else was willing to deal with. Who in my life is particularly difficult to love—who may God be asking me to love more now?
4. Thérèse did her chores cheerfully and willingly. What blocks me from doing my tasks with the same spirit? What motivates me to do my tasks with the same spirit?
5. What good work or act of compassion has been on my mind and heart that I haven't gotten to? What has been stopping me, and how can I use Thérèse's example to take my next step forward?
6. Dr. Gary Chapman wrote a bestseller called *The Five Love Languages*. He contends that each of us has a primary way we need to be loved by others. It can be words of affirmation, acts of service, physical touch, tangible gifts, or quality time. What is my primary love language? What do I think is the love language of my spouse or other key person in my life? Do I love that person in his/her language? How can I love that person better?

Suggested Actions

- Recite Thérèse's Act of Oblation to Merciful Love (see appendix 2).
- Celebrate Holy Mass.
- Spend time before the Blessed Sacrament.
- Reach out to someone who needs your special love.

Reflection Questions: Faustina (Hope)

1. In what ways have I been blocking God's mercy from fully healing me? What am I willing to do about that?
2. What in me prevents me from asking for forgiveness? Why do I think that is?
3. What in me prevents me from giving my forgiveness to another? Why do I think that is?
4. Faustina demonstrated great hope in the promises of Jesus. In what way do I consider myself a hopeful person? Where in my life can I provide more hope to a person or situation?
5. Can I name a specific person or situation in my life that I've written off as hopeless? When and how will I revisit that?
6. Was there a time when I, like Faustina, suffered a dark night in which I felt hopeless and abandoned? How do I feel recalling that occasion now?
7. When I feel hopeless, where do I turn for comfort?

Suggested Actions

- Pray the Chaplet of Divine Mercy, preferably during the Hour of Mercy, 3:00 p.m.
- Contemplate Christ's passion (private meditation or Stations of the Cross).
- Celebrate the Sacrament of Reconciliation.
- Offer someone forgiveness.

Reflection Questions: **Bernadette** *(Faith)*

1. In the early stages of the apparitions, the pastor of Lourdes rejected Bernadette. When has the Church or a particular priest caused me to feel hurt or abandoned?
2. Bernadette endured impoverished conditions and the ridicule of her peers in order to receive Holy Communion. How fervent is my desire to receive Holy Communion? What obstacles would I be willing to overcome to receive it?
3. In the convent, Bernadette felt isolated, misunderstood, and just plain different. When in my life have I felt that way?
4. When have I triumphed in taking a leap of faith? How does recalling that occasion now make me feel?
5. Where may God be calling me now to deepen my faith, and how will I go about doing that?
6. Where do I think I need the most healing: physically, spiritually, or emotionally? Why? I invite Our Lady of Lourdes into this area of my life.

Suggested Actions

- Pray the Rosary.
- Receive the Eucharist an extra time this week.
- Visit someone who is sick.
- Make a pilgrimage to a local shrine.
- Select a day to fast and offer it for those who are hungry.

APPENDIX TWO:
PRAYERS

Act of Oblation to Merciful Love

Offering of Myself as a Victim of Holocaust to God's Merciful Love

O My God! Most Blessed Trinity, I desire to Love you and make you Loved, to work for the glory of Holy Church by saving souls on earth and liberating those suffering in purgatory. I desire to accomplish your will perfectly and to reach the degree of glory you have prepared for me in your Kingdom. I desire, in a word, to be saint, but I feel my helplessness and I beg you, O my God! to be yourself my Sanctity!

Since you loved me so much as to give me your only Son as my Savior and my Spouse, the infinite treasures of his merits are mine. I offer them to you with gladness, begging you to look upon me only in the Face of Jesus and in his heart burning with Love.

I offer you, too, all the merits of the saints (in heaven and on earth), their acts of Love, and those of the holy angels. Finally, I offer you, O Blessed Trinity! the Love and merits of the Blessed Virgin, my dear Mother. It is to her I abandon my offering, begging her to present it to you. Her Divine Son, my beloved Spouse, told us in the days of his mortal life: "Whatsoever you ask the Father in my name he will give it to you!" I am certain, then, that you will grant my desires; I know, O my God! that the more you want to give, the more you make us desire. I feel in my heart immense desires and it is with confidence I ask you to come and take possession of my soul. Ah! I cannot receive Holy Communion as often as I desire, but, Lord, are you not all-powerful? Remain in me as in a tabernacle and never separate yourself from your little victim.

I want to console you for the ingratitude of the wicked, and I beg of you to take away my freedom to displease you. If through weakness I sometimes fall, may your Divine Glance cleanse my soul immediately, consuming all my imperfections like the fire that transforms everything into itself.

I thank you, O my God! for all the graces you have granted me, especially the grace of making me pass through the crucible of suffering. It is with joy I shall contemplate you on the Last Day carrying the sceptre of your Cross. Since you deigned to give me a share in this very precious Cross, I hope in heaven to resemble you and to see shining in my glorified body the sacred stigmata of your Passion.

After earth's exile, I hope to go and enjoy you in the Fatherland, but I do not want to lay up merits for heaven. I want to work for your Love alone with the one purpose of pleasing you, consoling your Sacred Heart, and saving souls who will love You eternally.

In the evening of this life, I shall appear before you with empty hands, for I do not ask you, Lord, to count my works. All our justice is stained in your eyes. I wish, then, to be clothed in your own Justice and to receive from your Love the eternal possession of yourself. I want no other Throne, no other Crown but you, my Beloved!

Time is nothing in your eyes, and a single day is like a thousand years. You can, then, in one instant prepare me to appear before you.

In order to live in one single act of perfect Love, *I offer myself as a victim of holocaust to your Merciful Love*, asking you to consume me incessantly, allowing the waves of infinite tenderness shut up within you to overflow into my soul, and that thus I may become a martyr of your Love, O my God!

May this martyrdom, after having prepared me to appear before you, finally cause me to die and may my soul take its flight without any delay into the eternal embrace of your Merciful Love.

I want, O my Beloved, at each beat of my heart to renew this offering to you an infinite number of times, until the shadows having disappeared I may be able to tell you of my Love in an Eternal face to face!

> Marie-Françoise-Thérèse of the Child Jesus and the
> Holy Face, unworthy Carmelite religious. This 9th
> day of June, Feast of the Most Holy Trinity, In the
> year of grace, 1895

Chaplet of Divine Mercy

1. Make the Sign of the Cross
In the name of the Father, and of the Son, and of the Holy Spirit. Amen.

2. Optional Opening Prayers
You expired, Jesus, but the source of life gushed forth for souls, and the ocean of mercy opened up for the whole world. O Fount of Life, unfathomable Divine Mercy, envelop the whole world and empty yourself out upon us. O Blood and Water, which gushed forth from the Heart of Jesus as a fountain of Mercy for us, I trust in you!

3. Say the Our Father
Our Father, Who art in heaven, hallowed be thy name; thy kingdom come; thy will be done on earth as it is in heaven. Give us this day our daily bread; and forgive us our trespasses as we forgive those who trespass against us; and lead us not into temptation, but deliver us from evil. Amen.

4. Say the Hail Mary
Hail Mary, full of grace. The Lord is with thee. Blessed art thou amongst women, and blessed is the fruit of thy womb, Jesus. Holy Mary, Mother of God, pray for us sinners, now and at the hour of our death. Amen.

5. Say the Apostles' Creed
I believe in God, the Father almighty, Creator of heaven and earth, and in Jesus Christ, his only Son, our Lord, who was

conceived by the Holy Spirit, born of the Virgin Mary, suffered under Pontius Pilate, was crucified, died and was buried; he descended into hell; on the third day he rose again from the dead; he ascended into heaven, and is seated at the right hand of God the Father almighty; from there he will come to judge the living and the dead. I believe in the Holy Spirit, the holy catholic Church, the communion of saints, the forgiveness of sins, the resurrection of the body, and life everlasting. Amen.

6. Say the Eternal Father
Eternal Father, I offer you the Body and Blood, Soul and Divinity of your Dearly Beloved Son, Our Lord, Jesus Christ, in atonement for our sins and those of the whole world.

7. Say For the Sake of His Sorrowful Passion
On the ten small beads of each decade, say this prayer: For the sake of his sorrowful Passion, have mercy on us and on the whole world.

8. Repeat for the Remaining Decades
Say the Eternal Father prayer (see number 6) on the Our Father bead and then ten prayers (For the Sake of His Sorrowful Passion [see number 7]) on the following Hail Mary beads.

9. Conclude with Holy God (Repeat three times)
Holy God, Holy Mighty One, Holy Immortal One, have mercy on us and on the whole world.

10. Optional Closing Prayer
Eternal God, in whom mercy is endless and the treasury of compassion—inexhaustible, look kindly upon us and increase your mercy in us, that in difficult moments we might not despair nor become despondent, but with great confidence submit ourselves to your holy will, which is Love and Mercy itself.

Sources

Kowalska, Maria Faustina. *Diary of Saint Maria Faustina H. Kowalska: Divine Mercy in My Soul*. Stockbridge, MA: Marian Press, 2003.

McEachern, Patricia. *A Holy Life: The Writings of St. Bernadette of Lourdes*. San Francisco: Ignatius Press, 2005.

O'Mahony, Christopher. *St. Therese of Lisieux by Those Who Knew Her*. San Francisco: Ignatius Press, 1975.

Pius XI, "Decree on the heroic nature of the virtues of the Venerable Sister Marie-Bernard Soubirous." Rome, November 1923.

Therese of Lisieux. *Story of a Soul: The Autobiography of St. Therese of Lisieux*. Translated by John Clarke. Washington: ICS Publications, 1996.

Elizabeth Ficocelli is a bestselling, award-winning author of fifteen books for adults and young people. Her books include *Seven from Heaven, Shower of Heavenly Roses,* and *Lourdes.* She has been published in numerous Catholic magazines such as *Columbia, America, St. Anthony Messenger,* and *Liguorian.* Ficocelli is a frequent guest on EWTN TV programs and on Catholic radio. She is also the host of *Answering the Call* on her local St. Gabriel Catholic Radio, in which she interviews priests, deacons, and religious about their vocations. She is also a popular national speaker at conferences, parishes, schools, and retreats. Ficocelli is a convert and the mother of four boys. She and her husband live in Columbus, Ohio. For more information, please visit www. elizabethficocelli.com.

For a complete listing of titles from

Ave Maria Press

Sorin Books

Forest of Peace

Christian Classics

visit www.avemariapress.com

 **ave maria press**® / Notre Dame, IN 46556
A Ministry of the United States Province of Holy Cross